LifeForce

*A Dynamic Plan for Health,
Vitality, and Weight Loss*

by

Jeffrey S. McCombs, D.C.

Robert D. Reed Publishers • San Francisco, CA

Robert D. Reed Publishers
P.O. Box 1992
Bandon, OR 97411
Phone: 650-994-6570 • Fax: -6579
E-mail: 4bobreed@msn.com
web site: www.rdrpublishers.com

Typesetter: **Barbara Kruger**
Cover designer: **Steven Scatliffe**

ISBN 1-885003-97-8

Library of Congress Control Number 2001090964

Manufactured, typeset and printed in the United States of America

This book is dedicated to

the potential that

lies hidden within

all of us

Acknowledgments

To my father who taught me to heal,
    Through the gift of his life and his death.

To my mother who teaches me to endure,
    And keep my faith.

To Terry, Kim, and Kelly, who share with me in all that I am and do.

To my friends and teachers—J-R, John Morton, John M., Fletcher, Jon, Saint, and Patrick.

To Victor Frank, DC, Ed Wagner, DC, and Robin Hyman, DC, who at one time or another, through their example, friendship and guidance, have inspired me to go beyond the surface, to explore, to challenge, to question, to think for myself and to forget what's accepted, in order to reach higher to find that which is possible.

To all of my patients who gave me the opportunity to make a difference in their lives, and they in mine.

To God and Christ,
    You have rolled away the stone from my tomb
    So that I might live again.

For all your love and support: Linda Joy, Tracy, Sandy, Denne, Andra, Nicholas, Jerish, Jesse, Wayne, Julia, Olivia, Morgan, Scout, Leslie, Tom, Kim, William, Shannon, Teri, Gina, Chrissy, Howard, Cliff, Fred, and Bai Hua.

To Virginia, for all your guidance and assistance in bringing this book about.

To Ana Maria, for all your loving and the gift of who you are to me.

You all have my undying love and gratitude.

Contents

Preface

The LifeForce Plan is a simple and effective approach that so many of my patients and others have used to rid their bodies of disease, illness and other health concerns. It is a successful tool for detoxifying the body, re-establishing the normal flora of the tissues, and re-awakening the body's innate ability to regulate, balance, and protect itself. It allows us to activate the endless life-force potential that resides in every cell of our bodies. Its somewhat seemingly miraculous results are achieved through a time-proven approach to reversing the ravaging effects that antibiotics have produced in our world today. Though antibiotics have a place, it is their overuse, misused abuse that produce a devastating imbalance in the body. The LifeForce Plan reverses that imbalance and restores the regenerative, life-enhancing cycle of the body, as the dominant cycle over the degenerative, "aging" cycle. It succeeds where other anti-candida diets have continuously failed, due to key fundamental insights. It also provides a way to balance the effects of antibiotics when their judicious use is necessary. It is not intended to be another "diet" book as such, but rather a way to achieve better biofeedback from the body that will enable you to make better dietary choices that work for you. It is a "bridge" back to an optimal state of health for your body.

"THE LIFEFORCE PLAN"

"YES" FOODS: All meats (except pork), vegetables, fruits (except oranges), eggs, brown rice, rice cakes (plain), hot brown rice cereal (plain), tea, coffee.

For cooking or salad dressing, we recommend using cold-pressed olive, apricot or almond oils (most other oils are toxic to the body). Seasonings include: Bragg's Liquid Amino Acids, salt, pepper, etc. (as long as there are no sugars, yeast, or anything not allowed on the PLAN. **We recommend naturally raised and organic foods**

"NO" FOODS: Anything not in the "YES" group is not on the PLAN. This includes all sugars (malts, honey, syrups, etc.), yeast, dairy, all grains (except brown rice), dried fruit, fruit juices, sweet vegetable juices, nuts, legumes, popcorn, soy sauce, vinegar, alcohol, breads, pastas, chips, milk substitutes, seeds, etc.

WATER: We recommend 1 quart of **purified water** per 50 lbs. of body weight per day. (e.g., 3 quarts of water per day if you weigh 150 lbs.).

SUPPLEMENTS: Candida Force – take 5 capsules, 3x/day between meals or at least 20 minutes away from food, for the first 8 weeks. **Detox Essentials** – take 4 capsules, 2x/day anytime but preferably away from the Candida Force, for the entire Plan. Supplements are available through your doctor or at lifeforceplan.com.

SWEATING: The major detoxification organs of the body are the liver, lungs, GI tract and skin. Fungal Candida increases the toxicity of the entire body and thus overloads the detoxification system. Therefore, it becomes essential to detoxify the body through its largest detoxification organ—the skin. **Exercise sweating doesn't count.** It is best to sweat 6x/week (30 minute hot baths or 10-20 minute saunas) We recommend 1-2 cups of Masada Salts with baths to aid in detoxifying the body. **Please note:** If you fail to follow the sweating protocol, your body will experience what may look like a cold, sore throat, etc., due to its attempts to detoxify the body through already overloaded systems. **THE SWEATING MUST BE DONE!!!**

THE LIFEFORCE PLAN (continued)

THE SCHEDULE

For best results, follow the program as outlined for 16 weeks. Beginning with week 7, you will need to begin supplementing the Plan with **Flora Prime** Acidophilus. We recommend taking this product with the dosage as follows:

- **Flora Prime.** Take 5 capsules, 2x/day, in between meals, weeks 7-16.

Note: The Flora Prime is available through your doctor or lifeforceplan.com. Flora Prime should be refrigerated to maintain potency.

The acidophilus bacteria is needed to reestablish the normal tissue flora in the digestive tract and throughout the entire body. Taking acidophilus prior to the 7th week provides only symptomatic relief. There is no room for the acidophilus to establish itself and grow in the digestive tract until the 7th week due to the overabundance of fungal Candida. Keep Acidophilus capsules refrigerated.

- Beginning with WEEK 9, you may ADD BACK—Dried fruit, juices, soy sauce, vinegar, legumes, nuts, and popcorn. KEEP SWEATING
- Beginning with WEEK 11, you may ADD BACK—Grains. SWEAT
- Beginning with WEEK 13, you may ADD BACK—Yeast. SWEAT
- Beginning with WEEK 15, you may ADD BACK—Sugars. SWEAT
- Beginning with WEEK 17, you may ADD BACK—Dairy. SWEAT

It may be necessary to delay adding sugars and dairy for a few additional weeks if your body is still sensitive to these foods. **Listen to your body! DON'T DO THE DIET, IF YOU DON'T DO THE SWEATING!**

CLOSING REMARKS

The best way to approach "THE LIFEFORCE PLAN" is by preparing large portions of meals in advance. Keep the appropriate foods and snacks handy. Remember your motto is "If in doubt, don't eat it." **You will experience a great increase in health and vitality if you follow "The LifeForce Plan"!**

(Pages viii and ix may be photocopied for your convenience.)

1

Change Your Life With the LifeForce Plan

I was beginning to give up hope, and I thought I would apply for disability benefits—this "rebirth" is nothing short of a miracle!
—*Janet, a patient, 1999*

The LifeForce Plan was "born" in 1993, while working with a patient who had come to see me for help with multiple symptoms and health concerns. Elizabeth told me that she hadn't felt well in many years and was living, as she put it, "half a life." Even worse, she was embarrassed that the parade of medical specialists she had seen over the years had come to think of her as a hypochondriac. Sometimes she thought these professionals might be right. After all she had so many symptoms, but no consistent diagnosis. There seemed to be no explanation for the way she felt most of the time. Maybe it was "all in her head."

During her first office visit Elizabeth described aching joints, almost daily headaches, irregular menstruation, digestive difficulties, steady weight gain, food allergies, insomnia, and increasing periods of depression. Clearly, her life had become a daily struggle. Ultimately, I determined that a condition known as systemic candidiasis was the underlying cause of these symptoms. Many other healthcare professionals and I believe that *systemic candidiasis* is an extremely common condition, but equally important, it is frequently overlooked, so it often goes untreated.

Systemic candidiasis is not well understood by most conventional medical practitioners and many are reluctant to recognize it as a common cause of ill health. The condition produces a diverse array of symptoms that affect numerous systems within the body. It's no wonder that it looks like a complex multi-system diagnostic "puzzle." However, once the condition is understood and identified, I have found that it is not difficult to treat. After less than two weeks of following the regimen that soon evolved into the LifeForce Plan, Elizabeth's symptoms had dramatically improved. About three months after her first office visit, she said:

"I had forgotten that it was possible to feel so good. For years, I struggled to get through the day, and I used various medications to mask the symptoms as best I could. The best thing about being on this particular healing journey is that now I wake up in the morning and actually look forward to the day!"

Over the next several years, I began to see an increasing number of patients with a host of diverse symptoms. And just like Elizabeth, these individuals began to feel better almost immediately once they started the LifeForce Plan. Diet is a key part of the LifeForce Plan, but I don't call it a "diet," because it is so much more. It contains six key components, all of which are explained in detail in the next chapter. The first stage, the basic plan, lasts eight weeks, and the next phase is an additional twelve weeks. So, in less than six months, men and women, some of whom have almost lost hope of ever feeling good again, find themselves with what several patients have called "a brand new life."

Renewed Vitality—A New Lease on Life

I like to describe the LifeForce Plan as a path to renewed vitality, which is why it feels like a "new lease on life." Do you remember how you felt as a young child? You were probably active and filled with energy. You knew when you were tired, and you fell asleep quickly and slept soundly; when you awakened in the morning, you felt renewed and refreshed. The LifeForce Plan may help you reclaim that same kind of vitality, as it has for so many patients at the LifeForce Center.

Many people tell me that they want "more energy," and I understand that they are tired of being tired. However, what is usually lacking is better described as *vitality,* the kind of vitality they had as children. Chronic illness or sub-par health robs us of the underlying vitality that fuels our spirit as well as our body. And there's a difference between feeling energetic and being filled with vitality. A shot of caffeine or even a candy bar can provide a jolt of temporary energy. As you probably know, that kind of energy is here one minute and gone the next. Only ongoing good health can insure your continued vitality. I call this program the LifeForce Plan precisely because of its potential to strengthen and renew your vitality—*your life force.*

Systemic candidiasis gradually robs its victims of their good health as it weakens the body's innate ability to heal and restore balance. Unfortunately, this condition, so pervasive in modern society, may do its destructive work for years before it is recognized. Even more unfortunate, it may *never* be diagnosed, but its consequences appear over a lifetime. The person who "just" has poor digestion, chronic headaches, poor concentration, difficult menstrual periods, low energy, achy joints, a host of other health complaints, may have undiagnosed systemic candidiasis. Too often, people view these symptoms as separate and unrelated, yet they may stem from the same problem.

Why You Should Be Aware of Candidiasis

You may be familiar with the term "candida," and you may think of it as a yeast infection. **Candida albicans**, a form of yeast, is one of the many microorganisms that normally exist in the body. When the internal bacterial environment in your body is in proper balance, candida remains in yeast form and is not problematic. However, when the internal bacterial environment is out of balance, candida cells may mutate into a fungal or **mycelial** form, which, over time, is potentially damaging to your health. *Mycelial candida* cells are able to "pierce" or invade the small intestine, thereby entering the bloodstream and spreading throughout the body.

Mycelial candida releases about *eighty* toxins per cell. So, multiply this by billions of candida cells present in the body and you can begin to see how a massive toxic overload can occur. Of course, the body has built-in defense mechanisms designed to handle the many toxins we are exposed to in a typical day. The lymphatic system is a primary channel to clear toxins from the body, but this normally efficient system can become overloaded. If you think of the lymph glands as forming a complex internal "sewer system," then you can imagine what happens when the system must work harder and harder just to keep up with continuous release of "waste." Eventually, the system becomes blocked—backed up—and the toxins that continue to be released by each cell are unable to drain from the body through the lymphatic system.

Over time, the lymphatic system will become overburdened, first by the presence of candida colonies, and then by the normal cellular waste products. This creates great stress on the detoxification pathways and organs, including the liver. Candidiasis, the overgrowth or over-abundance of mycelial candida cells, has the potential to create numerous symptoms—many dozens, in fact. However, to keep the issue simple, consider that the symptoms influence various body systems. In my practice, patients often report the following difficulties:

—**digestive problems:** constipation, diarrhea, the so-called "leaky gut" syndrome, and the symptoms associated with irritable bowel syndrome and colitis.

—**endocrine (hormonal) systems:** menstrual difficulties, infertility, vaginal yeast infections, sexual difficulties, and so forth. This category also includes diabetes and weight control issues. Food cravings are common, too.

—**urinary tract:** prostatitis, enlarged prostate, and urinary tract infections (in both men and women).

—**psychological health:** depression, lack of mental clarity, "fogginess," anxiety, emotional control, inability to concentrate.

—**immune system:** frequent colds and infections, but also autoimmune disorders such as lupus and scleroderma. Chronic fatigue syndrome is also common now, as are allergies and environmental sensitivities. Some men and women have been told they have multiple chemical sensitivity (MCS).

—**musculoskeletal system:** joint pain and swelling, and in some cases a previous diagnosis of arthritis, fibromyalgia, and so forth.

—**skin conditions:** fungal infections, rashes, dermatitis, psoriasis, eczema, and so forth.

Many people also complain of frequent headaches and fatigue, along with lack of stamina for exercise and often, sleep disturbances as well. These symptoms are typically associated with stress and many people try to handle these symptoms with stress management techniques. Unfortunately, improvement is temporary and uneven because the underlying issue remains unaddressed.

Another area that candidiasis can affect is the heart muscle and the lung tissues. This type of damage to the cardiovascular system is often undiagnosed, but it has been documented during autopsy following a cardiac event.

It is sad but true that many men and women with symptoms caused by candidiasis have been told that their problems are most likely psychosomatic in origin. When the true cause of a problem remains undiscovered, patients are often told in so many words, "it's all in your head." And like Elizabeth, some patients may begin to believe it.

Think of mycelial candida cells as tiny organisms that multiply rapidly and create havoc in the body because they invade and "take over" territory normally occupied by beneficial flora. Tragically, the multisystem havoc is almost always overlooked in conventional medical practices using standard diagnostic tests. Most medical doctors acknowledge that candida exists in many forms, but they fail to recognize *systemic candidiasis*. By that I mean the typical medical doctor does not link the array of diverse symptoms reported by so many patients with the disruption of the balance of microorganisms throughout the body. Unfortunately, because of specific conditions of modern life, systemic candidiasis has the potential to affect almost everyone in our society to one degree or another.

The Early Pioneers

The concept of systemic candidiasis is a relatively recent arrival in the healthcare world. A physician in Birmingham, Alabama, C. Orian Truss, is generally credited for bringing attention to this condition which, from the beginning, was viewed as a modern problem. In the early 1960s, Dr. Truss began to suspect the presence of a troublesome form of fungal yeast and over the next two decades he investigated *candida albicans (c.albicans)*. To this day, Dr. Truss' work remains a foundation upon which practitioners continue to build. Two other physicians, William G. Crook and John Parks Trowbridge, helped popularize the issue and inform the public about ways to treat it. Although I do not necessarily agree with all the treatment recommendations offered since the early 1980s when systemic candidiasis began to be widely discussed, these physicians are recognized pioneers in one of the most critical healthcare issues of our time.

A Thoroughly Modern Condition

Logically, one could ask why candidiasis has become a problem in the second half of the twentieth century and will continue to be a major health concern in the next century. Using the simplest explanation, there is a one-word answer: *antibiotics.* We can add steroid medications and oral contraceptives, but antibiotics are the primary culprits affecting men, women, and children across the planet, but particularly in Western societies where antibiotics are used so frequently—and often unnecessarily.

From the earliest days of antibiotic research and development, scientists recognized that antibacterial substances upset the balance of intestinal flora. As they "sweep" through the body killing microbes, antibiotic medications do not discriminate between harmful and beneficial bacteria. For example, antibiotics destroy acidophilus and lactobacillus, which are beneficial bacteria—the gatekeepers of the body's health and vitality. Simultaneously, antibiotics leave behind resistant bacteria, viruses, parasites, and yeasts. In the presence of antibiotics and the other substances that interfere with normal intestinal flora, mycelial candida cells rapidly begin reproducing and forming new colonies within the body. (The role of antibiotics in modern life and the consequences of their over-use are such critical issues that I included a more comprehensive discussion in a separate chapter.)

Once the process is underway, the candida cells find sustenance in many forms. For example, the typical U.S. diet contains numerous yeast-based products and fermented foods. Candida cells also thrive on sugar. Bread, vinegar, beer, wine, sugar-laden products such as ice cream, cake, cookies, and commercial salad dressings and sauces are daily dietary fare for many millions of Americans. Under normal circumstances, small amounts of some of these foods, while not necessarily health-promoting, may not be particularly harmful.

However, if systemic candida has taken hold in the body, then these foods continue to fuel the condition, potentially causing—and aggravating—symptoms.

Could So Much Poor Health Be Related to Candida?

Elizabeth was the first patient to use an early version of the LifeForce Plan. Since she improved so rapidly, I was encouraged to suggest the plan to other patients. When their health improved, too, it confirmed what many other health practitioners believe: *Candidiasis is a widespread problem, brought on by antibiotics and perpetuated through a combination of lifestyle and diet and an increasingly toxic environment.* Dr. Abraham Hoffer, one of the leaders in the field of orthomolecular psychiatry (a branch of psychiatry known for using specific nutrients to treat mental illnesses, such as schizophrenia) has estimated that one third of the world's population may be affected by candidiasis. I would add that most of the 33 percent is probably located in the industrialized world where exposure to antibiotics begins early and continues throughout life.

Clinical tests are available to diagnose candidiasis, although many physicians are not aware of them, nor do they necessarily believe in the efficacy of the condition—or the testing. Candidiasis also can be diagnosed using Applied Kinesiology (AK), which is the technique I used to diagnose Elizabeth. Some medical practitioners use self-report surveys, although these may help determine the severity of the symptoms more than actually providing a diagnosis.

I am not convinced that extensive testing is necessary, and instead am guided in my practice by the following principles:

1) **Most adults in the U.S., and children, too, have been treated with antibiotics, usually many different kinds.** Some individuals have taken antibiotics over extended periods for specific reasons, such as a way to treat stubborn acne. Millions of women have taken oral contraceptives, and millions of men and women have been treated with steroidal medications, such as cortisone-based formulations and prednisone.

2) **Exposure to antibiotics and other drugs has opened a pathway for candidiasis to take hold and produce its myriad symptoms.** While the degree of severity of these symptoms varies, almost every

person who comes to my office shows some evidence that candidiasis is present and causing symptoms.

3) **The LifeForce Plan is a safe, health building plan that detoxifies the body and promotes vitality.** There is nothing artificial or unnatural about the plan and the only expense it involves is the cost of three nutritional supplements and one specially formulated anti-fungal supplement available over the counter.

4) **Men and women who stick with the plan almost always begin to feel better, usually within the first week or two.** After three or four weeks, even those who have felt miserable and bothered by a host of symptoms experience significant improvement.

5) **The LifeForce Plan strengthens the immune system and revitalizes the body's innate healing mechanisms.** Because it leads to greater vitality and enhanced psychological well-being, I believe the LifeForce Plan helps delay the onset of many symptoms associated with growing older and usually considered signs of "normal" aging.

Taken together, the advantages of the LifeForce Plan are so great that there is no reason not to try this safe, economical, and effective program.

The Many "Faces" of Candidiasis

As previously mentioned, candidiasis produces any number of symptoms, from lethargy, fatigue, food cravings, and depression, to menstrual irregularities and/or infertility in women, to prostatitis and impotence in men. When you look at these symptoms listed as a group, they may look somewhat serious and are certainly hard to overlook. However, when considered one by one, as they often are in medical practice, they look like a "normal" or even "average" type of problem. After all, many women have irregular periods and are tired a lot, and infertility, while not normal, is not uncommon either. Many older men begin to have difficulties with prostate enlargement and urinary tract difficulties. Unfortunately, there is a tendency to accept many troublesome symptoms as "just a part of life."

Many of the digestive complaints diagnosed and treated by various types of healthcare practitioners are often related to candida. These include leaky gut syndrome (one consequence of long-term digestive problems), heartburn and reflux disease, weight problems, flatulence, and constipation, often alternating with bouts of diarrhea. In addition, candidiasis may produce skin conditions and pain and swelling in the joints, which may be misdiagnosed and treated as osteoarthritis. Muscle pain and weakness may be dismissed as just ordinary "aches and pains" that accompany aging. In actuality, none of these symptoms should ever be considered part of "normal" aging. Numerous symptoms are attributed to "only" stress, including headaches, skin conditions, food cravings, anxiety, and problems with forgetfulness or "fuzzy thinking." When taken together, these look like an impressive array of troubles! And it's all about stress?

By the time people hear about my practice and the LifeForce Plan, they may have been evaluated and treated by numerous specialists. In addition, some of these individuals have been told they have one of the many illnesses that produce a variety of symptoms, such as fibromyalgia or chronic fatigue syndrome (CFS), or even adult attention deficit disorder (ADD). Unfortunately, by the time I see these men and women, they also may be very discouraged—even hopeless.

Frank was such a patient. In his late forties, he looked much older, and he certainly felt older than his years. He had a chronic backache and pain between his shoulder blades. Tired all the time, with sinusitis and difficulty breathing, he was especially upset because he had developed incontinence, an inability to control urination. He had seen medical doctors and chiropractors and had been told that he had CFS. In addition to the physical symptoms, he felt increasingly withdrawn and had no desire for a social life. Even his family had begun to accept his social isolation.

After three or four weeks on the LifeForce Plan, Frank felt physically better, but he told me that the most profound change appeared in his renewed sense of emotional well-being. He had regained an interest in other people, and at a family reunion, some of his relatives hardly recognized him. He not only looked healthier, but he happily engaged with relatives who remembered him as withdrawn and depressed.

Frank referred other people to me, one of whom was severely depressed and exhausted. The best way to describe Jim is as a "bear of a man," the kind of man I expected to have great vitality. Jim broke down and cried on his first visit because he felt so hopeless, but he stuck to the LifeForce Plan and his transition back to health was profound. In fact, within a few months, Jim left an unfulfilling job and started a business he'd dreamed about for years. He also got married, so to say that the LifeForce Plan changed his life is an understatement!

The LifeForce Plan does not isolate one kind of problem and address it individually. For example, many of the women who come to the LifeForce Center report menstrual irregularities and infertility. Because the LifeForce Plan improves overall health, menstrual difficulties often disappear, and for reasons not completely understood, problems related to reproductive health clear up, too. Several women eager to start a family became pregnant after reversing their health problems with the LifeForce Plan. These women and the fathers involved most certainly know that this can be a life-changing program.

Those Troubling Weight Issues

I have often been asked if the LifeForce Plan is an effective weight loss program. Because it is not designed to be a weight loss plan, I caution people against thinking of it that way. However, people who need to lose weight usually find that their unwanted pounds begin to disappear when they follow this diet. They also report that their food cravings, which can be very powerful, tend to subside or disappear.

One patient, a middle-aged man named Jeremy, had multiple health problems, including a pacemaker, a history of seizures, and severe obesity. Over the next few months, Jeremy lost a significant amount of weight. He lost weight at a more rapid pace than the accepted conventional wisdom tells us is safe. However, I believe that the body will retain fluid in the tissues in order to buffer toxins. The fat tissues that contain the toxins will not be burned as fuel because there is a resistance to releasing the toxins. The slow weight loss of no more than two pounds a week that is usually recommended is often a loss of muscle mass rather than of excess fluid and fat. (I realize that this is exactly the opposite of what is commonly accepted in the weight loss field.) As you will see, the LifeForce Plan is a detoxification plan and the toxins can be safely released and cleared from the body.

In my practice, I've seen people lose up to ten pounds per week for several weeks, and they feel better as time goes by. I believe this rapid weight loss and the increased sense of well-being result because toxins are safely removed from the body. Slow weight loss may actually make some people feel weaker and sicker, because they are losing muscle mass and the toxins are still held in the body.

Although I know it is difficult for obese individuals to think this way, the LifeForce Plan does not require that you count calories or fat grams, nor will you weigh and measure your food. The way to lose weight on the plan is to stick with it. Food cravings are a common symptom of candidiasis, and when the body is detoxifying, food cravings may intensify for a few days. However, if you follow all the elements of the plan, these cravings for sugar or starchy food will disappear because the fungus cells are dying off—remember that the food you are craving may be just what the fungus cells need to sustain themselves.

More important than the weight loss itself, however, is the fact that vitality increases. I have had patients who hadn't exercised in years, but after following the LifeForce Plan, they started to go out for long walks, or they took up tennis or skiing or learned to swim. The increased activity contributes to fitness, not just weight loss. Individuals with great vitality are physically fit, not just thin.

Because I've seen patients lose 100 pounds or more, it is easy to see this plan as a weight loss program. However, obesity is not the only reason to start the LifeForce Plan, even though it may be a positive "side effect."

Those Aching Joints

Joint pain, sometimes accompanied by swelling, seems to show up often in patients with candida problems. When the body is overly toxic, and therefore producing many symptoms, the space around the joints often becomes filled with fluids containing toxins. In a sense, the joint tissues are "safer" depositories for toxins than a channel such as the liver, which is a primary detoxification organ. Unfortunately, the toxins cause inflammation, which eventually leads to joint tissue breakdown.

I have seen many patients who had been diagnosed with arthritis, which means "inflammation of the joint." Usually, these patients believe that the diagnosis is permanent and that the arthritis will progress. However, with the LifeForce Plan, the toxins are released from all the body's tissues, including the joints. Many patients find that their overall aches and pains go away, and those who have been troubled with joint pains are pleasantly surprised when the discomfort gradually disappears. In some people, joint mobility also returns as the fluid drains from the joints.

A Family Affair

Over the last few years, I've had the opportunity to help members of the same family regain their health. Fortunately, the LifeForce Plan can be "seductive." If you are close to someone who has had numerous health complaints, and now that person is profoundly changed, you may want some of that "magic," too. This is the reason I count families among my patients. (It also does not hurt that the LifeForce Plan involves eating *real* food, and any sense of deprivation is over in a matter of a few days—a few weeks at the most.)

In one case, a woman named Margo came to me because she was trying to stay well while coping with scleroderma, a serious autoimmune disease. She also needed to lose some weight and food cravings had been a problem for years. While she still has scleroderma, her symptoms have not progressed and if she sticks to the diet, she feels better. She has also been able to stay away from the steroidal drugs that are part of the conventional treatment for scleroderma. For Margo, the LifeForce Plan is ideally a lifelong plan.

After Margo began to improve, I saw her daughter and her husband, and soon, one of her sisters became a patient because she wanted help with migraine headaches, allergies, and fatigue. When she improved, her "worn-out" husband wanted to feel better, too, so he started the plan and it wasn't long before he felt as if he'd been handed a new life.

It is especially gratifying to treat couples and their children because the younger generation in these families has a head start in many ways. Most parents complain that their children prefer "junk food" to *real* food, but many children may not have better choices offered to them. In my experience, children who are exposed to the LifeForce Plan way of eating generally are healthier than many of their peers. Perhaps most important for long-term health, they lose their desire for the less healthful foods. Meanwhile, their parents are better educated about the folly of using antibiotics for all the colds and sore throats, and other infections common among children. So, rather than being overexposed to the number one cause of systemic candidiasis, these children may avoid the problem altogether.

It's Time to Get Started

By now, I hope you have a basic understanding of the underlying cause of numerous symptoms and health complaints. I cannot guarantee that you will never develop an illness, even a serious one. However, I can tell you that the LifeForce Plan offers you a chance to reverse some health problems you may have had for many years. It also offers you a chance for renewal. Like many of my patients, you may find yourself with renewed vitality and a new zest for life. That is certainly my hope for you.

Systemic candidiasis is a pervasive problem, and the LifeForce Plan is an effective way to treat it and rid yourself of its negative effects. In the next chapter, you will find an explanation of the six-part LifeForce Plan—you can begin this program and your personal renewal without delay.

2

Starting the LifeForce Plan

"The LifeForce Plan was the foundation for improving my health and preparing my body to heal from chronic fatigue syndrome."
—*Eric, a patient and professional model*

Given the effectiveness of the LifeForce Plan, you may assume that it is complex and difficult to follow. However, prepare to be pleasantly surprised by how easily you can integrate the diet into your life. Patients who have followed special diets for allergies, for example, or those who have tried other candidiasis programs are often amazed by the simplicity of the LifeForce Plan.

Note: *You will notice that a few products are described, along with dosage instructions. I recommend these specific products because I have found them to be the most effective and they are a critical part of the plan. I do not produce these supplements and other items, nor do I have any proprietary interest in them. You can find these products in health food stores, through mail order catalogs, or company websites. You can also order them from the LifeForce Center. Complete information about sources for these supplies is found in the Appendix.*

Begin At the Beginning

The LifeForce Plan is a basic **eight-week plan** and involves **six key components:**

- **the diet,**
- **a sweating regimen,**
- **water consumption,**
- **anti-fungal supplement,**
- **detox supplement, and**
- **acidophilus supplement.**

The first six weeks of the plan are identical, with changes occurring at Week 7 and again at Week 9. The diet then changes gradually for approximately the next ten weeks as you add foods back into the diet if so desired.

Beyond the eight-week basic plan, the changes are guided by your individual needs, usually based on the way you feel and how your body reacts to reintroduced foods. For example, while the diet allows sugars to be eased back in the diet, beginning with week fifteen, many patients decide to wait a few more weeks. Or, because they feel so good, they decide to leave most sugars alone permanently. After all, refined white sugar, corn syrup, honey, and other sweeteners are not essential for building or maintaining your health.

Virtually anyone can begin this plan. *Continue to take any routine medications. After you begin feeling better, you may discuss discontinuing or lowering the dosage of your medications with your physician. For now, however, do not take yourself off of prescription medication. The only exceptions are oral contraceptives and estrogen hormone therapy. Women should discuss alternatives to these medications to use for the duration of the program, but they must not stop using these drugs without talking with their physicians.*

To gain the maximum benefit from the program, follow these basic guidelines:

- **All six components are necessary.** *If you decide you are not motivated to drink all the water or schedule regular sweating sessions, do not begin at all.* Your body will detoxify and the water, the supplements, and the sweating serve to make that detoxification as effortless as possible as well as avoiding any long-term problems caused by toxic overload.
- **Choose a time to begin when your schedule for the first weeks is relatively routine.** By that I mean that you don't have travel plans or will not need to rely on restaurant food. (Once you

are established with the plan, you will be able to eat in many restaurants without difficulty.) However, do not wait for the "perfect" moment—it will never arrive. You will soon see how easily this plan fits into your life.

- **The vast majority of individuals experience no adverse die-off symptoms as a result of the body's detoxification process.** Virtually every person who has tried the diet begins to feel better, which increases motivation to continue.
- **Look for subtle changes in the way you feel.** The LifeForce Plan renews and revitalizes. You will notice an increase in your vitality, not just your energy. If you have been troubled by joint pains, headaches, indigestion, lethargy, depression, and a host of other symptoms, you may notice gradual improvement. However, some people notice a more dramatic reversal of symptoms. I cannot predict the rapidity with which your symptoms will reverse.

A Bounty of Healthful Food

Many food plans or diets begin by listing the foods you must eliminate, but I prefer to approach the LifeForce Plan in a more positive way. Let's look at all the foods I encourage you to eat. Plan your daily meals from the following categories of foods:

- **All meat, poultry, and fish, except pork. Yes, this means pot roast, steak, lamb chops, roast turkey, broiled chicken, duck, shrimp, salmon, and so forth.** Eggs are allowed, although I tend to advise patients to eat more egg whites than yolks. If you live in an area where game is available, you can have that, too, as well as domestic variety meats, such as buffalo, which has become available in recent years. Pork protein is difficult for the body to break down and digest and the fat in pork causes joint problems and neurohormonal imbalances in some people. In addition, pork cells contain—hold—viruses. For these reasons, pork is not allowed in the diet.
- **Virtually all vegetables and fruits are part of the plan.** Raw, steamed, or sautéed in a stir-fry main dish, you can eat freely from the wide range of produce available in supermarkets and health food stores. *Oranges are the only exception because they contain many types of fungi, which is why I removed them from allowed foods.* Orange juice is a staple

food in the U.S., but, unfortunately, the fungi make their way to the juice. Many people get a regular "shot" of fungal matter every morning with their supposedly healthful orange juice.

- **Brown rice, brown rice cakes, and cooked brown rice cereal are allowed.** Whole grain rice is a complete, neutral grain and is easily absorbed by the body. Plain brown rice cakes (no sugar added) are available in health food stores and some supermarkets. Be sure not to confuse the standard rice cakes with the real thing, brown rice cakes. Several brands of brown rice cereal are available and these are also allowed for those who enjoy hot cereal for breakfast. Oatmeal can be irritating to the colon and white rice does not help to synthesize B-complex vitamins, so it is of limited value. Many other grains cause mucous production in the digestive tract because of allergic reactions.

- **Olive, apricot, and almond oil are allowed.** I advise avoiding the heat-processed oils that have had certain key components removed. Removing these components extends the shelf life of the oil product, but processing affects how the oils are used by the body. Oils become rancid through a chemical process called lipid peroxidation, and rancid oils are toxic to the body. Buy oils in small quantities and if you find that you've stored open bottles of oil for several weeks, throw them out.

- **Use standard seasonings such as salt and pepper and various herbs and spices, such as parsley, chive, oregano, basil, thyme, garlic, and so forth.** A product called Bragg's Liquid Amino Acids tastes much like soy sauce and can be used as a seasoning.

- **Coffee, green and black tea, and herb tea are allowed.**

These are the basic foods around which you can build your diet. As you can see, no one is hungry on this diet.

The Short List

The list of what is not allowed on the LifeForce diet is much shorter:

- Avoid sugar in various forms, including malts and honey. Dried fruits and fruit juices contain concentrated sugar and are not included in the plan. As you read labels, you will see that many commercially prepared foods contain various forms of sugar.

- Soy sauce, teriyaki sauce, vinegar, and products containing vinegar, such as barbecue sauce, are not allowed.
- Because grains (except brown rice) are removed from the diet, you will avoid all bread, crackers, and pasta. You will also avoid legumes, such as lentils and soybeans. Popcorn, pretzels, and all kinds of snack chips are also not allowed.
- Avoid all dairy products.
- Alcohol is not allowed on the plan.

As you can see, many commercial foods and certainly the "fast foods" found on almost every corner across the country—and more recently, the world—are not part of the plan. Almost all commercial salad dressings contain vinegar and sugar so you will avoid them, too. (Olive oil with some lemon or lime juice is a good substitute salad dressing.)

But, But, But...

"Veterans" of candida-fighting diet plans are often surprised that on the LifeForce Plan fruit is not restricted and potatoes are allowed. In most plans designed to treat candidiasis starchy vegetables and fruits are restricted or eliminated. However, other programs do not use the candida-fighting formulation, Candida Force. This product kills the fungus so effectively that fruit sugar or the starchy vegetables do not cause problems, nor do these items slow progress. (Candida Force is discussed below.) So, with the exception of oranges, eat fruit and potatoes if you enjoy them.

Water, Water, and More Water

Many people drink very little water. In fact, many children are raised on sugary juice mixes and soft drinks. Too many adults use coffee or tea to start the day, they gulp down soft drinks all afternoon, and switch to beer and wine in the evening. Water is an afterthought at best. However, your attitude is going to change because water is an essential part of the LifeForce Plan.

Your body will be going through several weeks of detoxification, and water is key to making this a pleasant and healthful process. Water helps rid the body of toxins, but it also keeps every cell in the body hydrated. For optimal health your blood needs to be well hydrated, too. Dehydrated blood becomes abnormally thick, which forces the heart to work harder because the dehydrated cells of the heart muscle pump blood that is thicker than normal blood.

You must plan to drink *one quart of water (32 oz.) for every fifty pounds of body weight.* So, if you weigh 150 pounds, you will drink three quarts of water each day. If you are accustomed to drinking only two or three glasses of water a day—or even less—you will need to work up to the three or more quarts this plan requires. Just add a glass or so a day until you reach the appropriate amount. Once you begin to drink copious amounts of water, you will begin to lose your taste for sugary drinks and you won't reach for them out of habit in order to satisfy your chronic thirst.

What About Candida Force?

Earlier, I mentioned Candida Force, a substance that effectively kills fungal candida in the body. It is available through your doctor and manufactured for and available from lifeforceplan.com The LifeForce Plan calls for this specific formulation because it is the only anti-candida product I have found that effectively and safely kills the candida, as opposed to starving it out.

The primary ingredient in Candida Force is *undecenoic acid,* which is derived from castor bean oil; it is added to a base of olive oil (primarily). Candida Force works synergistically with the body and unlike other anti-candida products it has never produced harmful side effects. It will kill all the fungal candida, and if, for some reason, you continue to take the product beyond that point, it will not do any damage. Undecenoic acid also helps restore the normal tissue flora in the digestive tract.

The LifeForce Plan calls for *five Candida Force capsules three times a day, for a total of fifteen.* These capsules should be taken between meals or at least twenty minutes before or after eating. Children under age 8 should take 5 capsules, twice a day, for a total of 10.

The Detoxification Vitamin

The other nutritional supplement included in the beginning of this plan is vitamin C, and the product we use at The LifeForce Center and recommend to our patients is called **Detox Essentials,** produced specially for the LifeForce Plan. It is available through your doctor or at lifeforceplan.com

Based on my research and clinical experience, Detox Essentials is the most potent vitamin C available. As you may know, vitamin C is one of the important nutrients involved in promoting a healthy immune system and higher than normal doses of vitamin C will help the body handle the die-off of the candida fungus. Again, like the sweating and the diet, the Detox Essentials is a critical element in the plan.

Healing From the Inside Out

Detoxification puts a burden on the body. In order to maintain good health, or to recover from illnesses and rebuild and improve health, the channels through which the body clears toxins must be open and functional. The liver, the gastrointestinal (GI) tract, the lungs, and the skin are the major detoxification organs—or channels. Systemic candida overloads these channels, and places a particularly heavy burden on the liver and the gastrointestinal tract.

The LifeForce Plan, or any other detoxification program, adds to the toxic load already present, and can lead to unpleasant symptoms, such as headaches and fatigue. For this reason, the LifeForce Plan includes a regimen of induced sweating through either hot baths or dry sauna. Sweating takes the burden off the liver and the GI tract and takes advantage of the largest organ in the body, the skin.

Plan five to six "sweating sessions" a week. In a hot bath, it takes about 10 minutes for the body to begin to sweat and you should continue sweating for 10 to 15 minutes, so the baths are generally 25 to 30 minutes or more. Your bath water should feel hot rather than warm, but it should be comfortable and relaxing. Patients occasionally ask me how they will know they're sweating if they're immersed in water; however, your forehead and the back of your neck will become wet, so you'll know easily enough. Saunas usually provide heat quickly, and like baths, you should sweat 10 to 15 minutes, so your sauna sessions will be about 15 to 20 minutes. The recommended length of a sauna session assumes the sauna is the type generally found in health clubs and spas. Some saunas advertised for at-home use take longer to heat up, and in those, you may need to stay in a bit longer. (Always follow directions for safe use provided by a health club or included with your home sauna unit.)

For some reason, many people begin to think of all the reasons this is impossible, and some patients decide to just skip the baths or saunas. They soon begin to pay the price for overlooking this step. When the skin is not used for detoxification, the lungs will take over the job. Toxins will be excreted from the mucous membranes in the lungs, sinuses, and throat, and the symptoms resemble a cold with a sore throat. When patients experience these symptoms, they usually start the sweating protocol and the sore throat and other cold symptoms clear up. It isn't magic—it is the natural consequence of opening and using all the body's detoxification channels.

You may have greater access to hot baths than to saunas. You may be surprised that a hot bath can induce sweating because you are not accustomed to soaking long enough for the sweating process to begin. Perhaps your routine includes a quick daily shower and the idea of a hot bath sounds almost odd. Who has time for that? Well, make time. Some patients have told me that it had been years since they spent a half-hour doing nothing but relaxing in a tub! After Week 8 of the program, you can reduce your sweating baths to four to five times a week.

Bath salts may be helpful in clearing toxins from the body, but they are not necessary. The sweating is the most important thing. I have found that one product, Masada Salts, available in many health food stores, is the most effective in the detox process. Epsom salts are common and relatively inexpensive, but patients have told me that when they compared the bath water after using Masada salts and Epsom salts, the Masada salts produced "dirtier" bath water. This means, of course, that the Masada salts were more efficient in releasing toxins through the skin. Remember, however, that the sweating itself is the important element.

Exercise Is Not a Substitute for Sweating

A few of my patients thought they could skip the sweating protocol because they exercise regularly and always sweat during their exercise sessions. But I always warn these patients that the sweating that results from a fast run or walking or an aerobic exercise tape is not the same as the sweating that occurs during a dry sauna or a hot bath. The sweating that results from a hot bath or sauna involves conducting heat from outside the body to the core of the body, and toxins stored deeper within the body are released. Only sweating that is induced with a sauna or a hot bath will work to efficiently and effectively detoxify your body on this plan. If you avoid this step, you will likely develop *a sore throat and cold symptoms.*

Patients often ask about steam as a substitute for sauna. I don't recommend it because chlorine exposure is intensified in a steam room. However, if you have neither a bathtub nor a sauna available to you, then use steam to induce sweating.

Why Detoxification Is Important

It may be difficult to appreciate the critical nature of toxicity, and with it, the necessity for detoxification. We hear about toxins in the air we breathe and the water we drink, but we may not understand the extent to which we are exposed to toxins in modern society. The radiation we're exposed to is a toxin, and stress itself contributes to a toxic environment in the body. Add to that the overload of toxic substances in our food and even the fabrics we wear next to our skin and we can see why environmental toxicity is an ongoing concern.

You have heard about, or you may even have, one of the many conditions that are becoming more common. Fibromyalgia, increasing numbers of allergies, multiple chemical sensitivity (MCS), arthritis, lupus, and chronic fatigue syndrome (CFS) are related to the toxicity of the environment and the inability of the body to handle the onslaught of exposure to these toxins. These conditions are related to the inability of the immune system to protect the body from damage caused by the build-up of toxins. I also believe that the body goes through periodic detoxification, sometimes appearing as a common cold, in an attempt to clear toxins from the body.

It's Not Too Good To Be True

Some people look at the diet and immediately see that they will need to pass up their morning cereal with raisins and milk and the bread and roll basket at their favorite restaurant. And spaghetti dinners with red wine are out for the time being. However, others are amazed that pot roast and leg of lamb are back. Many people have banished red meat from their diets because they have been told that it contributes to heart disease. The new food pyramid emphasizes grains, beans, and legumes, and for many people, this has meant eating meatless pasta or bean dinners with highly processed bread products. So, here I come, adding to the current nutritional confusion by telling my patients that it is okay to return to the meat market and to the "good ol' days" when baked chicken or steak was an acceptable main course.

In a later chapter I discuss the current debate about low-fat, vegetarian-based diets versus adequate protein, lower-carbohydrate diets. I also include a section of recipes and menu ideas. For now, however, I simply encourage you to begin the plan and use your imagination to plan your meals. This is actually an "opulent" diet— choose spinach omelets, stir-fry meats and vegetables, roasts with vegetables, baked salmon fillets with dill, salads with a variety of greens and vegetables—even a buffalo burger if you wish—no bread, of course.

I recommend that you eat a wide variety of allowed foods in order to avoid becoming bored with the diet. However, there is no need to force yourself to eat zucchini if you prefer tomatoes. In other words, so many foods are included in the diet that there is no reason to eat foods you don't like. Certainly, we can develop tastes for foods, and white rice will seem bland once you acquire a taste for brown rice. I advise using the weeks on the LifeForce Plan as a time to both return to "old favorites" as well as to experiment with new foods.

The American Cancer Society's current dietary recommendations call for consuming a daily minimum of five servings of fruits and vegetables. The one thing that virtually all the major U.S. health societies and agencies agree on is that our population needs to increase its consumption of fruits and vegetables. As you can see, when you are on the LifeForce Plan, it is very easy to get the minimum servings. There are some high-protein, low-carb diets around that allow dairy products and pork, but few fruits and vegetables. These are not by definition anti-candida diets, however, so do not confuse them. They are not interchangeable, and besides, I encourage you to eat vegetables and fruit.

Another Step

After six weeks on the LifeForce Plan, you will begin taking acidophilus capsules before and after meals. At the LifeForce Center, we recommend one type:

Flora Prime—5 capsules, 2 times a day, 10-30 minutes before meals

I am often asked why I do not recommend taking acidophilus from the beginning of the plan. While the acidophilus bacteria are needed in order to restore the proper flora balance in the digestive tract, there is no room for the acidophilus to establish itself before about six weeks into the plan because there is an over-abundance of candida cells.

Another Look

Just to reiterate, here is a brief look at the plan:

1.   The diet, based on a foundation of meat, poultry, fish, fruits, and vegetables.

2.   The sweating regimen: six hot sweating baths, 30-40 minutes in duration, or, five to six sessions in a dry sauna for 10-20 minutes.

3.   Water consumption, one quart for every fifty pounds of body weight—purified water is best.

4.   Five Candida Force capsules, three times a day, between meals or at least 20 minutes away from food.

5.   Four Detox Essentials capsules, twice a day, anytime.

6.   After six weeks, add the acidophilus capsules as recommended, before meals.

Weeks Eight to Twenty

The remaining weeks on the LifeForce Diet involve a process of reintroducing foods. Listen to your body, however, and if you find that the foods do not agree with you or you have any type of adverse reaction, then remove them and try them again at a later time. The timetable is only valid *if you have followed the diet.* If you have had trouble with it and have gone off and on, then extend this timetable.

Beginning with **Week 9,** you may add dried fruit, fruit juice, soy sauce, vinegar, legumes, nuts, and popcorn.

At **Week 11,** you may add grains of your choice.

At **Week 13,** you may add yeast products.

At **Week 15,** you may add foods containing various forms of sugar.

At **Week 17,** you may add dairy foods.

You will continue to take the acidophilus supplement for a total of three to four months. After the thirteenth week, the Detox Essentials dosage can be reduced to four capsules a day.

These are basic guidelines, but listen to your body. You may need to delay adding sugars or dairy products if you are still sensitive to these foods. Some individuals decide to continue with the basic diet and eat the other foods, such as dairy or fruit juices or many grains, sparingly if at all. The fact is, most people feel very good while they're on the LifeForce Plan.

What To Expect

Motivation for staying with the plan is usually very high because many of the men and women who come to my office are tired of being sick—and tired. The hallmark of the LifeForce Plan is the absence of an adverse "die-off reaction," that is, symptoms associated with ridding the body of the candida cells. Rarely, a patient has so much candida fungus in the upper digestive tract that a die-off reaction occurs in the first few days. When this happens, I reduce intake of Candida Force to five capsules twice a day for three or four days and these individuals must sweat every day. However, as I said, this situation is rare.

At one time I thought it would take almost everyone about two weeks to "get with the program." However, many people clear their cabinets of the old food and bring in the new and that is that. Most patients experience very little difficulty, even during the first few days.

Some people may miss their glass of wine or their starchy or sugary snacks. Again, this is simply a matter of discipline early on. After a few days, most people no longer think about these foods. Eating in restaurants can be a bit of a challenge, but you will do well if you remember a few simple guidelines:

—Ask for sliced lemon or lime with your salad instead of dressing.

—Choose dishes in which it is easy to identify the ingredients: Grilled salmon, baked chicken, broiled sirloin, steamed vegetables, a green salad, and so forth.

—If you are stuck in a place with limited choices, order the burger without the bun or the turkey without the bread.

—Plain omelets and a fresh fruit cup—no added nuts or fruit juice—are safe choices.

—Ask for vegetables without sauces and make sure the baked potato is not covered in sour cream or butter.

—Most of all, enjoy yourself. There is no reason to isolate yourself from family and friends while you are on the LifeForce Plan. Continue a social life—you may feel more like being with other people because you feel so well.

Remember the Cause

In a very real sense, candidiasis is a problem brought on by "progress." While most of us cannot imagine life without antibiotics, they are not without adverse consequences. In the next chapter, I'll discuss the current problems brought about by the overuse of antibiotics. This will help you understand why and how you are affected by candidiasis.

3

The Antibiotic Dilemma

...Primum non nocera,
first, do no harm...
—from the Hippocratic Oath

"Unfortunately, we discovered that
bacteria are cagey, tenacious organisms
that swiftly developed resistance to
antibiotics... If left unchecked, antimicrobial resistance forebodes a global
public health crisis that threatens to return
mankind and the practice of medicine to
the pre-antibiotic era."
—Senator Bill Frist, M.D.

"...the emergence of drug resistance in bacteria, parasites, viruses,
and fungi is threatening to reverse medical progress of
the past 50 years...Today, we see a global resurgence of infectious
diseases such as tuberculosis and the rapid spread of antimicrobial
resistance. As we approach the twenty-first century, many important
drug choices for the treatment of common infections are becoming
increasingly limited and expensive and, in some cases, nonexistent."

These words do not come from someone who has an interest
in alarming the public. In fact, they are statements made by Dr.
David Satcher, who was then the Surgeon General of the U.S., on
February 25, 1999, during his testimony before the Senate

Subcommittee on Public Health. Dr. Satcher also provided the senators an overview of the problem of antimicrobial resistance, which is essentially the same information that I provide here.

In addition to Dr. Satcher, Dr. James Hughes, the Director of the National Center for Infectious Diseases, which is part of the CDC, the Centers for Disease Control and Prevention, also provided testimony about the current crisis we face. "We are facing a serious global problem of antimicrobial resistance," Dr. Hughes reported, "that affects virtually all the pathogens we have previously considered to be readily treatable." He also pointed out that most states do not require that drug-resistant infections be reported, which we can interpret to mean that the public may not be aware of the extent to which resistant infections have invaded specific communities.

Senator Bill Frist, quoted above, spent many years as a heart-lung transplant surgeon before he successfully ran for the U.S. Senate. At the hearing mentioned above, he stated that virtually *100 percent* of heart-lung transplant patients develop post-operative infections, and not only do these infections prolong hospital stays and increase costs, some of these transplant patients eventually die as a result of their infections.

Science Fiction or Science Fact?

In the novel *Deadly Indian Summer*, published in 1997, author Leonard Schonberg describes the threat of a deadly disease that modern medicine can't control. Eventually, in order to solve the "mystery" of the disease and save many lives, the protagonist, a young physician, must look beyond traditional medical assumptions and explore Navajo healing traditions. In another novel, *The Eleventh Plague*, published in 1998, authors John Marr and John Baldwin take on the issue of bioterrorism in order to illustrate that disease epidemics can no longer be considered tragedies we read about in history books. When Richard Preston wrote the chilling account of an outbreak of an Ebola virus in a U.S. lab in *The Hot Zone,* its drama gave it a sense of suspenseful fiction, but readers realized they were reading a true account.

Whether fact or fiction, these books remain popular because they explore a profound and deep fear. While we may not think about it every day, we know that we are vulnerable to diseases for which there are no cures. Sure, "miracle" drugs are touted in magazines and on television, but that does not mean that a modern version of the Black Plague isn't just around the corner. Novels and movies with disaster and epidemic themes are likely to increase in the coming years—life and art regularly imitate each other and true stories serve as the fuel that fires the imagination.

The Truth Is Indeed Stranger

Fiction aside, during the last few years disturbing news reports have surfaced about deadly bacterial strains that are resistant to existing antibiotics. One of the most ominous reports involves a lethal strain of *staphylococcus aureus,* which until recently was confined to hospital and nursing home environments (that seems ominous enough in itself). According to the news services, and confirmed by the Atlanta-based CDC, over two hundred people in Minnesota and North Dakota were infected with this type of bacteria—and *four children died.*

Health authorities were concerned because this bacterial strain had not caused deaths in the U.S., although deaths had been reported outside the country. Furthermore, at the time of these reports, great concern surfaced that the drug-resistant germ had spread, because the four children who died from the bacterial infection had not been hospitalized at the time they contracted the illness.

In 1995, there was only one antibiotic, vancomycin, available to treat *staphlycoccus aureus.* During that year, infectious disease specialists were concerned that when the bacterial strain became resistant to vancomycin, there were no more drugs left in the arsenal. And, the deaths from this particular staph strain were reported in 1997 and 1998, further adding to the concern.

During the winter of 1998, a similar situation developed in the Chicago area when eight deaths from infections were reported in the news. It seems these individuals also contracted an infection that was resistant to existing antibiotics. Some people express surprise along with dismay, but we must ask why anyone would be shocked by these incidents. We have had plenty of warning.

These incidents call attention to a much wider problem, which is the increase of antibiotic-resistant strains of bacteria. The phenomenon was not only predictable, it was documented during the earliest days of antibiotic research. We were given a clue about trouble ahead, but no one knew quite how serious the future problems might be.

You may have heard of Alexander Fleming, the man considered the "father" of antibiotics and hailed as a medical hero in the annals of the "fight against disease." Fleming first noted that introducing antibiotic substances to bacteria immediately resulted in resistant strains. While antibiotics undoubtedly have saved millions of lives, these medications produced numerous problems. These problems include the current epidemic of systemic candidiasis that remains for the most part an unacknowledged cause of widespread health complaints.

Some False Assumptions

In classrooms all over the country, school children are taught, in so many words, that the "war against infectious diseases is just about won." The image of "man against germs" is powerful, and most of us have been led to believe that germ-killing antibiotic drugs are a kind of super weapon that wiped out a host of serious diseases.

When we examine this issue more closely, however, it becomes apparent that antibiotics were added to the medical toolbox after the incidence of diseases such as pneumonia, diphtheria, scarlet fever, typhoid, and tuberculosis had already declined significantly. Antibiotics did not hasten their decline, nor did they significantly lower the death rate from these diseases. Rising standards of living and improved hygiene had more to do with advances in public health and lowering death rates from infectious diseases than the introduction of antibiotics.

Because of the misconceptions about the role of antibiotics in reducing incidence of infectious diseases, many healthcare professionals have been reluctant to take a hard look at the capacity of antibiotics to do great damage to health. Clearly, a balanced approach is lacking. Rather than looking at a range of possible treatments for particular illnesses, there has been a tendency to quickly pull out the prescription pad. This habit is so entrenched that some patients believe they have not received legitimate treatment if they leave a doctor's office without a prescription for something to "fight the infection." Patients often do not stop to think that the antibiotic they are given could be completely ineffective, either because the particular strain of bacteria is resistant to it or because the illness is caused by a virus. Remember, too, that antibiotics work in a specific way on specific types of germs; there is no such thing as a "one size fits all" antibiotic.

How Antibiotics Work

We are so used to thinking of antibiotics as "germ killers," that we may not understand how they work, or why they can cause trouble. Bacteria are single cell organisms that need other living organisms to sustain themselves, and billions of these cells take up residence in our bodies. Bacteria, like all living creatures, have a lifecycle, and they can produce a new generation every twenty minutes or so. To be effective, antibiotics must interfere in one stage or another of the lifecycle. Some antibiotics work to "confuse" bacteria by acting like natural substances with which the germs normally coexist. Some antibiotic substances interfere with proliferation by acting on the cell wall, thereby disrupting cell reproduction. Bacteria may mutate on their own, a phenomenon known as spontaneous mutation.

Just like movie monsters and fictional disease epidemics, however, the harder we try to get rid of harmful bacteria, the bigger and more threatening they become. You see, bacteria aren't stupid; in fact, just like all living things, they fight to survive, and they have great powers of adaptation and resilience. Kill a batch of staph bacteria with "antibiotic A," and the next batch of staph germs will have a new genetic structure that ignores drug "A." So drug "B" is developed, and soon the cunning germs mutate again and drug "B" is rendered ineffective—and then doctors are offered drug C.

Over the last fifty or sixty years, this process has repeated itself over and over again. The constant fight to stay one step ahead of the next powerful strain of bacteria is not always won. Today, there are drug-resistant strains of bacteria associated with tuberculosis (TB), pneumonia, strep, and staph. Furthermore, often it takes a higher dose of the antibiotic to rid the body of the infection. This is the reason that news reports about deadly infections give rise to fears about the national and global health issues.

Few people give tuberculosis more than a passing thought, especially in the U.S. However, TB is on the rise, and what is more critical to this relatively recent comeback, large numbers of recent cases (from the mid-'80s through the '90s) are labeled MDR, which stands for multi-drug resistant.

MDR-TB is such an important example of the consequences of bacterial adaptation because TB is an airborne infection, most often settling in the lungs. Anyone who breathes air containing these bacteria can become infected. Obviously, not everyone will become ill, and individuals who are exposed to the same bacteria are not equally susceptible. "Latent tuberculosis infection" means that the tuberculosis bacillus is present in the body, and otherwise healthy individuals may not become ill. However, to rid the body of the infection, it is believed that treatment with an antibiotic drug is necessary. But in the case of MDR-TB, no drug is available to treat the disease. It is estimated that *10-15 million* individuals in the U.S. carry latent TB infection, with about 1-1.5 million likely to become ill during their lifetime. No one can say for sure how many of these men, women, and children will die, but mortality rates for MDR-TB run between 70 to over 90 percent. Many millions of people are infected worldwide, so one can only imagine the impact MDR-TB could have on global health.

For too long, we have harbored—even nurtured—a kind of arrogance that we can beat nature at its own game. We are rapidly learning, however, that fighting wars against disease is not always the best way to protect our health. The fact is, over 500 pathogens live in the body, and between 300 and 400 coexist in the intestinal tract alone. Our best bet against disease is to protect rather than destroy the natural but delicate balance that protects our health.

Reaping What We Sow

A crisis in healthcare exists today in part because patients and their doctors have formed a kind of unspoken alliance. The lay public has become accustomed to thinking that infections are *supposed* to be treated with antibiotics. For example, a family physician could say, "You need rest, plenty of water, and some remedies designed to strengthen your immune system. I'll take a culture and then if it turns out this is a bacterial infection and an antibiotic is needed, I'll know which one is likely to be effective."

This process takes longer, and too often is bypassed by prescribing an antibiotic before it is even established that the infection is bacterial rather than viral. And because doctors have tended to think that antibiotics can cure infections so easily, they rarely mention botanical or nutritional therapies that may also help the immune system resist the infection.

Taking an antibiotic unnecessarily has often been viewed as inconsequential. However, when we introduce an antibiotic substance into the body, this increases the risk of then developing a different infection. The new infection may be resistant to the antibiotic designed to treat that type of bacteria. In other words, we eliminate a possible treatment for another unrelated infection. Any time we introduce a drug that acts on an organism in the body, we change the nature of the organism. There is no way around that fact.

Most common colds and flu are caused by viruses and not bacteria, so many of the millions of antibiotic prescriptions written every year are useless, and because they cause bacterial mutations, they may actually cause harm. When I think about the overuse of antibiotics, I am reminded of the famous phrase in the Hippocratic oath: *Primum non nocera,* or, *first, do no harm.* At one time, almost everyone was ignorant of the long-term adverse effects of the overuse of antibiotics. Nowadays, however, no health professional can claim ignorance about the adverse consequences of misusing antibiotics. The indiscriminate use of antibiotics harms individual patients and threatens to adversely affect global health. Medical authorities themselves continue to issue warnings about this problem.

Just How Overused Are Antibiotics?

Antibiotics are prescribed by most medical specialties, but some types of practices use them in great numbers. For example, pediatricians and family practice physicians diagnose ear infections among children. Ear infections, many of them caused by viruses, are among the most common childhood infections. A *half billion dollars* worth of antibiotics are prescribed every year just to treat childhood ear infections. About the same amount of money is spent to treat other childhood infections. There appears to be no leveling off of these numbers, because between 1980 and the early to mid-1990s, the number of prescriptions for antibiotics written for children doubled.

What makes this even more outrageous is the fact that *viruses,* not bacteria, cause more than *90 percent* of infections in children.

The problem of overuse is not new. In fact, in the early 1980s, it was estimated that over half the adults who saw physicians with common cold symptoms, were given unnecessary antibiotics. Overall, the medical community reached a consensus that 40 or 50 percent of antibiotic prescriptions are unnecessary—and that's a conservative estimate.

Fifty million pounds of antibiotic drugs are produced annually, which represent about 235 million doses. If close to half of these doses are unnecessary, we can see that there is a tremendous economic toll of this careless practice. Antibiotic overuse is costly in ways that may not be immediately apparent. For example, in his opening statement at the aforementioned February 1999 Senate hearing, Senator Frist stated that about *30 billion dollars* are annually spent on the cumulative effects of antimicrobial resistance.

Where We're Heading

Ironically, when resistant bacteria strains develop, there also is an increased incidence of infectious illness. Ear infections among children have actually increased in number over the last few decades. In Dallas, Texas, researchers examined circumstances around an outbreak of a penicillin-resistant infection among already hospitalized children. The children infected by the bacteria were more than twice as likely to have been treated with an antibiotic during the preceding month. In other words, antibiotics weakened immunity among these children, thereby making them more susceptible when exposed to a new bacterial strain.

Hospitals are prime breeding grounds for resistant strains of bacteria. This increases the odds for contracting infections in the hospital, which are termed "nosocomial infections." You may also have heard the term, "iatrogenic illness," which means an illness that results from a medical treatment. Illnesses resulting directly from a drug—or any other medical treatment—are examples of iatrogenic illness; infections brought about by compromised immunity resulting from the overuse of antibiotics represent another example.

The CDC has estimated that in the U.S., about two million hospital patients develop a nosocomial infection every year, and even more alarming, close to *90 thousand* of these patients die as a result of the infections. The human toll is huge, but the financial toll is great as well. These hospital-acquired infections cost consumers about *4.5 billion dollars* each year—and that number is likely to rise along with all other healthcare costs.

From Normal to Toxic

You have probably heard about serious health concerns caused by *E. coli,* and the problems are linked to undercooked ground meat sold in restaurant settings. What you may not realize is that *E. coli* is one of the normal intestinal microorganisms. For decades, fast food restaurants have served hamburgers and *E. coli* did not cause problems. But, this particular bacterial organism has been repeatedly exposed to antibiotics, and it has mutated, thereby creating new forms now linked to serious adverse effects.

Once new drug resistant bacterial strains develop, they enter the environment along with all the other bacteria present. So, when you take an antibiotic that alters the bacteria causing your infection, your family becomes exposed to the new strain too, and although they may not become ill, they are carriers of the infection and may pass it on to others.

Killing the Good Along With the Bad

The *E. coli* story and many others illustrate various long-term consequences of antibiotics. As I explained in chapter 1, antibiotics upset the balance of health-building intestinal flora, the microorganisms essential for health. Since the early days of antibiotic use, healthcare practitioners have known that antibiotics can lead to yeast infections, which are essentially the overabundance of yeast cells in relationship to other microorganisms. While treating a bladder infection, for example, the common antibiotics also kill off the bacteria that help keep yeast cells in normal levels.

Vaginal yeast infections, so common among women, occur when the normal bacteria in the moist vaginal tissues are destroyed, often because a course of antibiotic treatment was given for an infection elsewhere in the body. Yeast infections represent a noticeable sign of imbalance in the body, but most candidiasis goes unnoticed. Once the mycelial—fungal—form of the naturally occurring yeasts becomes established, it can lead to suppressed immunity, which leaves the body vulnerable to a wide range of conditions, including other infections.

We have already discussed the many potential symptoms produced by systemic candidiasis, and I mentioned that patients have come to me after receiving a diagnosis of chronic fatigue syndrome (CFS). Carol Jessup, M.D., who has conducted research into CFS, determined that among one group of patients she observed, 80 percent had a history of repeated antibiotic use.

Some individuals, mostly teenagers of both sexes and young-adult women, have been given low dose antibiotic treatment (usually tetracycline) to treat acne. Some women are given the antibiotics to counteract the skin problems caused by oral contraceptives, which are also implicated in the development of candidiasis. A type of oral contraceptive exists that includes a low dose of tetracycline, and in television ads it claims to promote radiant skin while acting as a contraceptive! This is another example of iatrogenic illness, although it is still not recognized as such.

Although some healthcare providers consider systemic candidiasis widespread and, perhaps even more important, an *authentic* illness, many conventional practitioners do not. Therefore, little if any consideration is given to the potential long-term adverse effects of the conditions that lead to candidiasis. But I know from my practice, that this illness causes incredible suffering.

Red Flags—Be Alert

All major medical organizations in this country and throughout the world have recognized the serious nature of drug-resistant bacteria. Therefore, *casual* use of these drugs is no longer justified. In actuality, it never was justified, but now there is no excuse. You can find out if your doctor is aware of the seriousness of misuse and overuse of antibiotics because he or she should be aware of current CDC guidelines for antibiotic use. These guidelines include the following basic principles:

- Antibiotics should not be prescribed over the phone or following only a brief examination.
- Children who are relatively healthy should not be given antibiotics for minor infections. There are natural ways to

treat many infections, including those occurring in the ear. Ask about alternative treatments and if your doctor does not ever offer any, find another family physician.

- If you question the necessity for antibiotics, your doctor should take your concerns seriously. If your questions are brushed aside or you are told the drug is harmless, seek help elsewhere.
- Does your doctor take cultures? Much antibiotic misuse occurs because the drug doesn't match the bacteria—and as we've seen, it is becoming increasingly difficult to find the right drug. Culturing bacteria should become a more common practice, not a less common one.
- Equally important, your doctor should demonstrate some knowledge of natural ways to boost immunity and resist infections and fight them off when necessary.

Research and Development

We find ourselves in this particular muddle because there has been no concerted effort to find alternatives to the many antibiotics manufactured by pharmaceutical companies. The second half of the twentieth century has been dominated by the "chemical" revolution. In medicine this has meant one new drug after another, and in the case of infectious disease, it's a matter of staying one step ahead of the next "smart germ." The race is being lost, however, but economic incentives continue to fuel drug research, while potential natural remedies for many human ills remain untested.

Millions of people are voting with their feet and are seeking primary care from physicians who practice holistic medicine or from other practitioners, such as chiropractors. I believe that chiropractors are a good choice for primary care, precisely because they turn first to natural remedies that work in harmony with the body. Chiropractic philosophy is rooted in maintaining health and building natural defenses against disease.

One way the current crisis in health care is going to be resolved is by patients educating themselves about the best way to protect their health. One important way to improve health and strengthen immunity is to safely treat systemic candidiasis with the LifeForce Plan. This is one step you can take to help your body strengthen immunity and reduce the need for antibiotic treatment.

The Word Is Out

You should never believe everything you read, including the information in this chapter, without careful consideration. Much of the data mentioned here are available on a government website. I have also listed books that further explain the current crisis in antibiotic use and guide you to the judicious use of natural remedies. When you do your own research, I think you, too, will be concerned about the global consequences of the misuse of antibiotics.

By now you have probably started the LifeForce Plan, and in the next chapter, I will elaborate on the way candidiasis affects the body and you'll learn more about the way the LifeForce Plan can help you.

4

Why the LifeForce Plan May Be Right for You

My hope for regaining my health is blossoming again. I am in much less pain. My body has shifted and I'm losing fat and wearing clothes I haven't worn in a long time. My skin has cleared and brightened, and I feel wonderful!
—Patti, a recent patient

The path patients follow to find the LifeForce Plan often resembles a maze. For the most part, the men and women I see come to me after making the rounds of medical specialists. Some have spent years looking for help, and many have spent thousands of dollars, too. Candidiasis is not a widely recognized condition, so therefore, few individuals are told they have it. Because the condition affects numerous biological systems, patients may be treated symptomatically, problem by problem. They take one drug for their headaches, another for allergies, and still another for joint pains, and so on. Women may be offered hormonal treatment for menstrual irregularity or infertility and both sexes may end up taking one of the many relatively new drugs for digestive symptoms. Many patients have extensive testing for a variety of health problems. Over the years, I've seen numerous individuals under treatment for both physical and psychological disorders. When one considers the type and number of symptoms that can appear when candidiasis is present, then it's no wonder that millions of people believe it's normal to take daily medications.

Since most patients have been through batteries of tests and have extensive medical histories, I have not found still more testing necessary in most cases. As I've said, I recommend the LifeForce Plan to virtually all my patients. Patients may tell me they have already been diagnosed with arthritis, fibromyalgia, allergies, infertility, and so forth, or they simply report a list of symptoms with many different diagnoses. Either way, I find that the LifeForce Plan offers relief, usually within a few days.

I understand that you may be skeptical when you hear about a single plan that offers benefits to almost everyone, regardless of the specific array of symptoms or diagnosis. However, the LifeForce Plan is fundamentally a detoxification diet, and virtually no one in our society can escape exposure to the conditions that produce candidiasis. This fact underscores my belief in the power of the plan to bring about dramatic improvement in all those who are willing to try it.

You can use this easy-to-follow plan based on the basic instructions outlined in chapter 2. This is possible because the LifeForce Plan is safe and has neither side effects nor risks associated with it. I decided to provide the list of widely reported symptoms associated with candidiasis because some people want this type of verification. If you've read other books about candidiasis, these lists will sound familiar, but I have not listed any symptom that I have not heard reported from my own patients. Remember, too, that any exposure to antibiotics in your life makes you a good candidate for the plan. So, if you have ever taken antibiotics or are experiencing *any* of these symptoms, I suggest that the LifeForce Plan is right for you.

In addition, you will notice that many of the symptoms and conditions listed are considered "part of life." Or, once you have a diagnosis, the problem may be labeled "chronic" and you may be told you have little choice but to control the symptoms and learn to live with the condition. For the most part, this is ridiculous. Every year, Americans spend billions of dollars on doctor visits and medications that do nothing more than controlling and masking the symptoms of conditions they have been led to believe are chronic. I can think of no good reason to accept unpleasant symptoms and do nothing to eliminate their root cause.

Digestive symptoms:

Constipation and/or diarrhea, colitis, leaky gut syndrome, chronic indigestion, and heartburn, gastritis and bloating, and acid reflux. You may be told you have irritable bowel syndrome (an inclusive term that covers a lot of ground) or diverticulosis or any number of digestive complaints. Patients are usually told these are chronic conditions and any number of over-the-counter and prescription drugs are recommended to relieve the painful and distressing symptoms. These drugs may accomplish that goal, which is part of "learning to live" with digestive conditions; seldom are these problems considered curable.

Allergy symptoms:

Headaches and dizziness, food and chemical sensitivities (usually increasing in number), various sensory disturbances (such as blurred vision and ringing in the ears), earaches, and asthma. Patients often undergo a variety of allergy tests. They are given lists of foods to avoid, often permanently. Chemical sensitivities may lead to social isolation because these individuals are bothered by common perfumes, exhaust fumes, cigarette smoke, and eventually, all kinds of common chemicals used in building materials and to make furniture and household products. Seasonal allergies are treated with medications. Men and women who suffer from regular headaches may take strong pain relieving drugs for many years. Like digestive disorders, allergies are often viewed as a "normal" part of life for some people.

Musculoskeletal symptoms:

Various body aches, joint pain and stiffness, and periodic muscle cramping and weakness. Conventional medicine offers a variety of diagnoses, most commonly osteoarthritis, and nowadays, fibromyalgia. If you are older, say, over 50, you may complain about body aches only to be told that you should expect to have aches and pains because you're moving right along toward old age! In addition, some musculoskeletal conditions are treated with corticosteroid drugs, such as Prednisone, which further depress the immune system. Pain relieving drugs and steroids always overwork detoxification pathways and exacerbate candidiasis.

Reproductive system and urinary tract:

In women: irregular menstrual cycles, heavy bleeding, menstrual cramping, and Premenstrual Syndrome (PMS), which incidentally has a long list of symptoms associated with it, many of which mimic candidiasis. Women may also report endometriosis, infertility, recurring vaginal yeast infections, frequent urinary tract infections (UTI), urinary incontinence, and diminished sex drive. Women generally are given treatments that address symptoms, and in the case of PMS, some lifestyle alterations are recommended. Unfortunately, treatment for urinary tract infections inevitably involves antibiotics. Some women end up taking several courses of antibiotics each year because of chronic UTIs. They then are treated for the vaginal yeast infections that develop because the antibiotics have interfered with the flora balance in the vaginal environment.

In men: frequent urinary tract infections, persistent fungal infections such as athlete's foot, benign prostate enlargement, prostatitis, diminished sex drive and sexual dysfunction. These conditions are treated symptomatically; infections are treated with antibiotics, which then worsen the candidiasis and increase the intensity of the symptoms.

Skin conditions:

Candidiasis produces odd rashes and skin eruptions and infections that have no obvious cause. In addition, conditions such as psoriasis and eczema also occur. Patients always report improvement in skin conditions after they start the LifeForce Plan. Unfortunately, many skin conditions are treated with antibiotics (usually tetracycline) or topical creams containing cortisone. Ultimately, these medications perpetuate and exacerbate candidiasis.

Psychological symptoms:

This category of symptoms includes the lethargy and fatigue many people with candidiasis report, but it also includes depression, insomnia and other sleep disturbances, memory problems, anxiety and nervousness, and an inability to concentrate. Many people talk about chronically low energy and overall apathy. Dozens and dozens of medications exist to treat these problems.

If you watch any television at all, you have seen commercials for medications to treat various types of mood disorders. Based on advertising dollars spent to promote these drugs, it's apparent that our society is plagued with digestive problems, headaches, muscle and joint pain, insomnia, and more recently, a host of psychological problems we are told to discuss with our doctor. After all, the pharmaceutical companies tell us that help is on the way. Of course, legitimate psychological conditions exist and I would never advise you to stop taking medications that have been prescribed for you. However, I also suggest that you start the LifeForce Plan. Over and over, I have seen many of these psychological symptoms improve as a result of the body's detoxification.

Miscellaneous symptoms:

Candidiasis can cause food cravings, usually for sweets and carbohydrate foods, and a tendency to gain weight. As I've said, The LifeForce Plan is not a weight loss diet. Fat cells tend to hold toxins in the body and toxins accumulate in fluids around the joints (a situation that leads to joint pain and stiffness). As the body detoxifies, it will begin burning fat. The plan does not require counting calories or carbohydrate grams and you needn't weigh and measure your food. The LifeForce Plan helps eliminate food cravings, which helps patients normalize their eating habits.

Our society has a high incidence of degenerative conditions, such as cardiovascular diseases, hypertension (high blood pressure), and diabetes. Although a genetic component exists, these conditions largely result from lifestyle, especially poor diet. The LifeForce Plan has the potential to help normalize blood fats and blood pressure. It helps you build a base of vibrant health that works to prevent degenerative diseases and musculoskeletal problems, such as arthritis and osteoporosis. If you can prevent the onset of the age-related degenerative conditions, you will have taken an important step in preserving your energy and well-being, even as the years accumulate. Aging doesn't have to be about medications and pain and loss of vitality.

Just Begin

I could continue talking about the types of illnesses that plague our population, and may even affect you. But it isn't necessary to do so. I suggest that you order the supplements and clear the food that is not allowed on the plan out of your refrigerator and kitchen cabinets. Start now, and give yourself a chance for better health. (As I've said, *do not stop current medications*.) Follow the plan as written and see what happens. Others have, and I assure you they are living happier, more vital lives today.

5

Unraveling Myths About Protein

"...what happens when we cut back our fat as the nutritional establishment recommends? Since we can't for the most part remove the fat from the food, we end up replacing foods that contain fat with those that don't. Most vegetable sources of protein—beans and grains—are incomplete unless combined carefully and contain far more carbohydrate than protein. In the end, if we strictly follow the low-fat prescription, we can end up deficient in protein."

—Michael Eades, M.D., and Mary Dan Eades, M.D.

As you have seen, the LifeForce Plan not only allows meat, poultry, eggs, fish, and game meats, the plan *encourages* a diet rich in protein. My approach to protein consumption differs from some current thinking about protein, but evidence exists that the low-fat craze may be coming to an end and protein may have its reputation restored. Nowadays the conventional wisdom dominating our airwaves and print media emphasizes the notion that the majority of Americans probably consume too much animal protein and fat.

Many health-conscious consumers have been led to believe that meeting the body's protein requirements can be accomplished so easily that they need not be concerned with it. However, I do not believe we should leave the job of consuming adequate protein to chance, nor do I think that haphazardly combining a variety of foods automatically results in "good enough" protein consumption. I begin this discussion of protein with a discussion of fat, because many dietary trends affecting protein consumption came about because of broad assumptions about the amount of fat found in the standard U.S. diet.

Your Confusion Is Justified

Consumers often complain about conflicting and confusing nutritional advice and information. Confusion is understandable because dietary advice often is presented as established fact, not supposition or theory—and relatively recent theory at that. However, much of the advice that appears in books and articles and on radio and television—and now on the Internet, too—is faulty and may even promote the diseases it purports to help prevent. Major medical societies endorse certain foods and put their "heart smart" seal of approval on them, which leads consumers to believe that the majority of research firmly supports including abundant amounts of these foods in the diet.

Unfortunately, the advice about which I speak builds on several current myths about protein and fat. For example, you probably have read or heard, perhaps from a healthcare professional, that fat consumption, in and of itself, contributes to many diseases, including various types of cancer, and in particular is implicated in increased incidence of cardiovascular diseases. Cardiovascular disease, or heart disease, is not a single entity, but rather a group of diseases; taken together, these diseases comprise the number one cause of death in the U.S. and other industrialized societies.

A corollary to the current advice is the belief that populations in Western cultures tend to consume more than required amounts of protein, and furthermore, plant proteins are superior to animal protein. Since protein and fat occur together in meat, dairy products, and so forth, one proposed solution to the excess fat consumption is to restrict animal protein. When we take away one type of food, we need to replace it with something else in order to meet even basic calorie requirements. Cutting back on animal protein consumption inevitably led to consuming more protein from vegetable sources.

Before coming to The LifeForce Center, many of my patients either adopted a vegetarian diet—at least to a degree—or they believed they *should* reduce animal protein foods in their diets. They may even become defensive and apologize for not "giving up" meat. Most show surprise when I tell them that vegetarians tend to be among the most unhealthy men and women who arrive looking for help from The LifeForce Center. Often, minimal consumption of usable protein in their diets has left them with an emaciated look.

Protein and fat issues are complex because they are intertwined. Perhaps you have heard that fats derived from animal sources are by their nature less healthful than fats derived from plant sources. The next "fact" presented usually concerns excessive fat intake, regardless of the type and source of the fat. If you look at the U.S. Department of Agriculture's new food pyramid you can see that it reinforces the notion that animal protein and fat are at the very least not particularly important for human health, and at worst, detrimental to health. According to the food pyramid proportions, the bulk of calories should come from carbohydrate foods, and it leaves the impression that protein requirements can be easily met with vegetable protein sources. While the pyramid does not totally eliminate animal protein, it explicitly and visually diminishes its benefits and value. Fats occupy the smallest place on the pyramid, and as a result, many people believe that small quantities of vegetable oils meet all requirements for fat in the diet.

Where Has All This "Good" Advice Brought Us?

After several decades of well-meaning advice to reduce fat and animal protein in the diet, we are left with some dismal facts. The emphasis on a low-fat, high carbohydrate diet has not resulted in decreased incidence of cardiovascular disease, and obesity rates have never been higher. In actuality, as Americans attempted to decrease fat in the diet, they added fat to their bodies.

Those who tout the high-carbohydrate, low-fat diet fail to warn consumers about how unhealthy it is to "virtuously" cut back on animal protein while consuming ever greater amounts of diet soft drinks and reduced fat and fat-free products. While obesity rates reach epidemic status in the United States, keep in mind that no other society fills its supermarket shelves with such a vast array of "diet" foods.

Millions of Americans wash down a "fat free" brownie with "sugar free" drinks and are puzzled as they watch the numbers on the scale rise. Ironically, the less animal protein and fat Americans eat, the heavier they get. Equally ironic, Americans have shifted away from animal fats toward greater consumption of vegetable oils, which has resulted in increased percentages of unhealthful partially hydrogenated fats in the typical diet.

While exact figures remain difficult to establish, according to current estimates approximately one-third of the U.S. population fit the medical definition of obesity, that is, they weigh at least *twenty percent* over their optimal weight. Anyone who has ever attempted to lose weight understands well the challenge involved in losing twenty percent of body weight. Even more alarming is the estimate coming from The Institute of Medicine of the National Academy of Sciences that *two-thirds* of Americans are overweight to some degree. Keep in mind that this trend started in the first half of the twentieth century, a period in which consumption of vegetable oils in the form of margarine and vegetable shortenings began its steady increase.

When Food Isn't Food

Any discussion of current dietary trends is incomplete without looking at the vast array of so-called fabricated foods that line the shelves of the typical grocery store. Along with efforts to reduce fat consumption, the "lite" craze began, which could legitimately be called the trend toward substituting phony or imitation food "products" for the real thing. For example, products called "cheese food" are not actually dairy products. Imitation sour cream is made with vegetable oil and numerous fillers; "whipped topping" cannot be called whipped cream because it is not made from heavy cream, but rather is a mixture of fillers and various chemicals made to look and vaguely taste like whipped cream. And the popular egg substitutes promoted as better for you than the real thing are actually fabricated from vegetable oils. Of course, these products don't carry a label that says: "You are buying a fabricated food."

At one time, margarine products, made from partially hydrogenated vegetable oils, were promoted as superior to butter. However, the process of hydrogenation, which turns a liquid vegetable oil into a solid fat such as shortening or margarine, increases the percentage of a type of fatty acid called *trans-fatty acids*.

The easiest way to describe trans-fatty acids is to say that they are produced when fat that is liquid at room temperature is hydrogenated, thereby altering its molecular structure to become solid at room temperature. Trans-fatty acids are incorporated in the cellular structure where they have the potential to interfere with efficient energy production and the body's system of manufacturing various hormones. Bear in mind that these hydrogenated and partially hydrogenated oils are ubiquitous in commercial foods from margarine and other fabricated dairy substitutes to baked goods.

At one time, trans-fatty acid consumption was relatively low, but with the advent of hydrogenated vegetable oils, the percentage of trans-fatty acids in the American diet has increased dramatically. The increase has been steady, too, as the multinational food manufacturing giants have promoted highly processed vegetable oils as superior to fat derived from animal sources.

Meant as an amusing example of the "huckster" mentality, Mark Twain told a strangely prophetic story in his book, *Life on the Mississippi*. Twain claims to have overheard two businessmen discussing their successful ventures. One man was making his fortune by passing off reconstituted cottonseed oil as high quality imported olive oil, and he boasted about the "ripping" business he enjoyed. The other man claimed bragging rights over the tons of cheap oleomargarine he sold as fast as his factory could produce it. He laughingly predicted that soon butter would disappear and imitation butter, his factory-produced oleo, would dominate the market. Think of this story the next time someone tries to tell you that imitation foods are just as good—and nutritionally sound—as the real thing.

Cholesterol Gets a Bad Name

For the past twenty or thirty years, theories about the cause of heart disease have focused on the "lipid theory," or put another way, the theoretical link between high blood cholesterol and cardiovascular disease. You may believe that the cholesterol theory is established fact now, but you would be mistaken. Fifty or sixty years of research have yielded conflicting and confusing results. The well-known Framingham study, often cited as the "premiere" long-term study of heart disease, failed to show a definitive link between high cholesterol levels and death rates from heart disease. However, some research suggests an increase in male death rates from all causes when cholesterol levels drop *below* 160 mg/dl.

Remember too, that scientists only began to devote considerable research dollars to various aspects of heart disease when rates began to rise in the United States during the post-World War II era, a time that vegetable oils gradually accounted for an increasing percentage of calories in the diet. Not coincidentally, this was also a period when consumption of heavily processed carbohydrate foods increased and consumers were dazzled with nonstop introduction of new snack and convenience foods. Many of these foods contain unhealthy forms of fat and large amounts of sugar. (Couple this with the steady rise in antibiotic use during the same era and it is easy to see that the stage was set for an epidemic increase of a variety of diseases.)

You should know that the major health organizations in the U.S. did not reach consensus easily and some scientists remain unconvinced about the role of fat in heart disease. Animal and human studies produced widely varying results and even population studies lack clarity. Some experts claim that societies whose diets are primarily vegetarian have low rates of heart disease when compared to meat-eating cultures. However, other experts point to the Eskimo and Inuit populations whose indigenous diet includes almost nothing other than protein and fat, but show almost a complete absence of heart disease. Tragically, signs of heart disease begin developing in Eskimo populations when they start consuming the carbohydrates found in the mainstream U.S. diet.

In the early 1970s, researcher George Mann reported findings of his studies of the Masai population in Africa. According to Mann, the Masai consume large amounts of cholesterol and saturated fats and have virtually no heart disease among their population. Mann had once been associated with the Framingham project but his ideas were at odds with the "lipid hypothesis" and eventually he referred to it as a scam.

In the dubious quest to reduce all types of fat in the diet, many people have unwisely reduced animal protein consumption to a point at which they may be protein deficient. However, protein is essential to optimal health, and protein deficient people are invariably tired and lethargic, not to mention vulnerable to an array of health problems.

The Truth About Protein

The word protein comes from the Greek word meaning "first importance," and the more we diminish its importance in the diet, the greater the risk of developing health problems. I base this statement on my own observations and on views of others who raise questions about the wisdom of the current low fat, high carbohydrate dietary trend.

In general, research about the importance of protein is clear, and inadequate protein intake has implications for whole populations. For example, protein intake has increased in the Japanese population over the past few generations, and as a result, average height has increased. It is not a coincidence that during this century, the Japanese population has consumed greater amounts of protein and also increased its consumption of animal protein. Japanese-Americans also grow taller than their ancestors and it is believed that the difference can be accounted for by greater amounts of protein in the diet. Because of the prior limitations in the diet, the Japanese population did not reach its hereditary potential. Consider this an example of just how important protein consumption is. Do we really want to be casual about the amount and quality of the protein we put on our tables?

Several authors have presented information exposing the disadvantages, even dangers, of high-carbohydrate, low-fat diets. In recent years numerous books have appeared that base weight-loss plans on reducing both refined and complex carbohydrates and increasing animal protein in the diet. While these plans often differ from one another, and they differ from The LifeForce Plan in substantial ways, I welcome any voice that exposes the misinformation about protein consumption to which most Americans are exposed.

Protein is more than one simple entity, so when we discuss protein, we probably should use the plural form because the body needs more than 100,000 different proteins. Amino acids are the basic building blocks of the protein molecule, and as you may know, some amino acids are called essential, while some are called non-essential.

Essential amino acids must be consumed from foods because the body cannot synthesize them. The nine essential amino acids are: histidine, isoleucine, leucine, lysine, methionine, phenylalanine, threonine, tryptophan, and valine. **Nonessential** amino acids are those that the body can synthesize—given the building blocks with which to do so. Cystine, taurine, and tyrosine are sometimes considered *conditionally essential* amino acids because situations exist in which the body cannot synthesize them in adequate amounts and they must be obtained from food.

Proteins also contain the elements oxygen, carbon, hydrogen, and nitrogen, and some protein molecules contain other elements such as heme-iron, found in hemoglobin, or iodine, found in thyroxin, the hormone produced by the thyroid gland. Specific proteins are formed by patterns of amino acids, and the nucleus of every cell contains a genetic code that determines the pattern.

The body is a collection of cells, of which the primary component or "ingredient" is protein. The membrane that surrounds the cell is comprised of protein, and protein is also found inside the cell. If you remember nothing else about protein, remember that the body constantly breaks down protein and replaces it. This is why you need adequate protein every day to maintain health. The body manufactures enzymes, antibodies and hormones, too, and requires protein for those processes. Your body needs protein in every stage of life, but in certain periods, such as childhood and adolescence and, for women, during pregnancy, more protein is required to meet the greater demands.

All Proteins Are Not Created Equal

Proteins vary in amino acid content and digestibility. Complete proteins, which contain all essential amino acids, have greater biologic value than incomplete proteins, which have varying amounts of only some essential amino acids. All amino acids must be supplied in adequate amounts, and *resupplied,* because when even one amino acid is missing, protein production stops. The essential amino acids cannot be stored for later use, but are broken down and used for energy. You may have heard that if your calorie intake is too low, your body will break down tissue to use for its needs. In a similar way, if protein intake is inadequate, the body will break down protein tissue in your organs to use for its needs. When individuals adopt a calorie-restricted diet in order to lose weight, it is especially important to consume adequate protein because the body will use muscle mass and even organ tissue to meet its own needs. Nowadays, weight loss plans that are comprised of primarily complex carbohydrates may lead to weight loss, at least some of the time. However, some of the pounds lost are actually sacrificed protein tissue, not fat tissue. When protein intake is inadequate, an elaborate system of compensation "kicks in," and the body enters a type of survival mode and struggles to maintain itself, using muscle and organ tissue if necessary.

Animal protein, which is similar to human protein tissue, is considered the highest quality protein because it contains all of the essential amino acids, although they appear in varying amounts in different animal protein sources. The soybean represents the only plant protein source that contains all nine essential amino acids. Other plant protein sources have a variable amino acid profile, but they lack adequate amounts of specific amino acids. The term *limiting amino acid* refers to the specific amino acid that is inadequate in a particular food. For example, wheat and rice do not contain adequate lysine and corn is limited in both lysine and tryptophan. Methionine is the limiting amino acid of legumes, including soybeans.

Soy and Complementary Proteins

When protein quality and amino acid content are mentioned, the discussion usually turns to issue of soy protein and its potential usefulness as an adequate substitute for animal protein. Generally, the experience of Asian populations is raised as proof that we don't really need animal protein in our diet. In addition, justification for this view usually continues by mentioning complementary proteins or protein combining.

Some vegetarian populations exist across the planet, although relatively few cultural groups are 100 percent vegetarian. Until recently, our society made animal protein, i.e., meat, poultry, fish, and dairy products, the centerpiece of the diet. A main dish was usually defined by its protein—chicken marsala, beef kabobs, grilled salmon, spring lamb stew. In actuality, for most Westerners, animal protein remains the featured attraction, but nowadays, many people feel guilty about their food preferences.

For numerous reasons, most of them completely erroneous, animal protein started to develop a bad reputation, starting in the 1960s and '70s, when data about the role of fat in the increasing incidence of heart disease began their journey of misinterpretation. Giving meat a bad reputation proved a difficult task. Most of us raised in the U.S. were taught in school about the importance of high quality protein and we associated this with meat and eggs and dairy products. Many people found it difficult to believe that plant protein could provide an equivalent substitute. They were correct to be skeptical.

Vegetarian populations tend to combine plant foods that contain what are known as complementary proteins, meaning that the amino acid content of two or more plant foods will complement each other to form a complete protein. The staple foods of many cultures rely on complementary proteins. In Mexico and Central America populations rely on corn and beans, for example, which contain complementary amino acids. Complete proteins, such as dairy or small amounts of meat usually are added to various dishes, so in reality, complementary proteins comprise only part of the diet.

The ability to be a healthy vegetarian is actually a genetic issue. Our bodies tend to better use and absorb the kind of protein to which we are genetically predisposed. Most of my patients trace their genetic roots to meat-eating cultures of Europe and elsewhere in the world. In addition, many patients whose genetic roots are in a variety of Asian, Middle Eastern, and African countries are accustomed to consuming animal protein, too, although these cultures may not have relied on it as heavily as Western cultures. I have had patients from India, or whose roots are Asian Indian, and some of these individuals have been exclusively vegetarian. Because of their genetic structure, they do not efficiently break down and absorb animal protein. For these individuals, a diet comprised of animal protein, vegetables, and fruit does not promote health. And, as an aside, a colleague of mine believes that it probably takes about twelve generations to turn an animal protein consumer into a vegetarian.

Can I Use This Protein?

If the amino acid content of protein were the only issue, then basic protein requirements likely could be met with careful planning. However, amino acids tell only part of the story about the needs for protein and about protein quality.

Digestibility is a key factor in determining the quality of a protein. In order to be absorbed and used by the body, a protein must be digestible, that is, broken down by digestive enzymes. Animal protein is considered more easily digestible than plant proteins because enzymes must break through cellulose that surround the protein in plant cells. As a child, you were probably told hundreds if not thousands of times to "chew your food," and the advice is as sound today as it ever was. Regardless of the source, well-chewed protein is more easily digested, and therefore more easily absorbed and used. Digestion starts in the mouth, not in the stomach.

You may have heard the popular saying, "You are what you eat." In reality, that saying should be changed to, "You are what you eat, digest, and most importantly, *absorb*." As you will see, you cannot absorb and use protein unless you regularly supply your body with high quality protein foods.

From a Steak To a Peptide

Peptides result from protein digestion and are called breakdown products. Protein must be "broken down" into amino acids to form peptides and individual peptides are comprised of two or three amino acids. Different types of peptides are formed in the stomach and small intestine. The body receives the products of protein digestion through the blood stream by way of the liver. The liver retains some amino acids to form various proteins found in the blood and it uses amino acids to form liver tissue.

Remember that the liver is the primary detoxification organ, and if it is overloaded and toxic itself, this limits its ability to produce plasma proteins. When this occurs, a major pathway of protein utilization is impaired. This is precisely what I see among patients with candidiasis, which produces myriad symptoms because the detoxification pathways, including the liver, are compromised.

Protein digestion and utilization are extremely complex physiological processes. However, keep in mind some key issues about your body's need for protein. First, your body doesn't store amino acids. The metabolic pool of amino acids found in every cell in your body are present and available to meet the continuous demands of your tissues. The cells of your body are never static, but rather are dynamic systems in which cells are broken down and replaced. The breakdown process is called *catabolism* and the replacement process is called *anabolism*. Some soft tissue cells undergo rapid breakdown and replacement, whereas bone cells are replaced more slowly.

Imbalances in protein intake have an immediate effect on the body, because protein intake must be adequate for the constant breakdown and replacement—protein turnover. Urea, creatinine, and uric acid are byproducts of protein metabolism and are excreted through the kidneys in urine. Amino acids are also excreted through sweat and feces. The body is continuously taking in fuel and breaking down and rebuilding tissue. Protein is the essential first component in this process.

Nitrogen is essential for life and proteins are the only source of nitrogen. The amount of nitrogen excreted in urine and feces is a good indication of how much protein the body has broken down. *Nitrogen balance* describes the state in which the amount of nitrogen obtained from protein foods equals the amount of nitrogen excreted from the body. A *positive* nitrogen balance occurs when more nitrogen is consumed in protein foods than is excreted. A positive nitrogen balance is needed for growth and therefore is seen in infants and growing children as well as in adolescents and during pregnancy.

Under certain circumstances, more nitrogen is excreted than consumed in protein foods, which means that protein tissues are broken down faster than they are replaced. This situation is called a *negative* nitrogen balance, and may result from numerous situations such as injury to the tissue or burns, along with illness and inactivity, but also when caloric intake is restricted. When the amount of protein ingested is either inadequate or the quality of the protein is poor, then the body's critical needs for essential amino acids are not met.

Severe injury and illness are situations in which tissue breakdown accelerates and negative nitrogen balance results. When we are ill, we tend to be inactive, which may lead to protein tissue loss that occurs when excreted nitrogen is not replaced in protein foods. You may have observed the loss of muscle tissue and tone among elderly people who gradually become less and less active.

What you are seeing is the shift in nitrogen balance, which leads to a decrease in muscle tissue. Regardless of age, a sick person's protein requirements may be about the same as the needs of a growing child or adolescent. Because of the prevailing assumption that most people consume adequate protein, few people pay enough attention to their need for protein. As a result of a casual attitude toward protein, many patients I see are actually protein deficient.

Protein's Many Jobs

Promoting growth and maintaining the integrity of the body's tissues are generally what most people know about protein. But the 100,000 proteins our body synthesizes have many functions. They are needed to transport nutrients in the body, particularly non-water soluble nutrients. Proteins called *lipoproteins* function as transporters of blood fats such as cholesterol and triglycerides. When protein is inadequate, cholesterol accumulates in the blood as well as in tissues in the body. Because proteins are "carriers" of certain vitamins and minerals, as well as lipids found in the blood, adequate protein intake is essential for detoxification. Rather than viewing elevated cholesterol levels as a signal to decrease animal protein, and hence, animal fats, I see the high numbers as a signal to increase protein.

Proteins also are essential for maintaining a balance of fluid in each cell. Plasma proteins are, as the name implies, proteins found in the blood. Plasma proteins are large molecules that remain in the blood, and these substances provide the mechanism by which fluid is drawn out of tissues rather than accumulating.

Edema, which is the accumulation of fluid in the cells, occurs when protein consumption is *inadequate.* However, when enough protein is consumed, then the tissues begin releasing accumulated fluids. This is one reason for the rapid weight loss I see among patients at The LifeForce Center. Within a few days of increasing protein in the diet, their protein-starved tissues are allowed to function normally again and the fluid imbalance is corrected. From what I see in my practice, mild edema is a very common condition, but often goes unnoticed.

While you probably never think about it, your body needs protein to maintain a favorable pH balance, which means a neutral or slightly alkaline state. Adequate proteins in the blood prevent the accumulation of acids, which would then shift the pH balance to a less favorable state.

You have no doubt heard of infection fighting substances called *antibodies*. Antibodies are proteins and in situations when protein consumption is inadequate, antibody production slows down. In other words, if you don't eat enough protein, you will become susceptible to infection and more likely to be affected by other toxic conditions. This is true in the development of candidiasis, which is essentially a toxic condition in the body. Protein is essential for detoxification, and since The LifeForce Plan encourages protein consumption, patients begin the detoxification process immediately.

The Dairy Question

While animal proteins supply essential amino acids, I make distinctions among some animal protein sources. For example, in the early weeks of The LifeForce Plan, dairy products are eliminated. For many people, milk is not the best protein source because it produces allergic reactions. In addition, milk is a concentrated source of pesticides and other toxins. Although dairy products may be added back to the diet, many of my patients find they feel much better after eliminating all dairy products. Eventually, most of my patients eat dairy products very sparingly, if at all. For those people who add dairy back to their diet, I recommend consuming products that are as close as possible to their original state (i.e., half-and-half instead of whole milk).

Unfortunately, many people believe that non-fat dry milk is a desirable food because it is an inexpensive complete protein source. However, it is an altered protein, and I do not believe the body utilizes it efficiently, and therefore, I do not consider it a reliable protein source.

Complete Proteins But Unhealthy Foods

Almost all non-dairy animal protein foods are allowed in The LifeForce Plan, and even dairy may be added back after several weeks. However, I recommend that you avoid eating liver because for all animals, the liver is the major detoxification organ.

Pork is the other animal protein I recommend my patients permanently eliminate from their diet. In recent years, reports have surfaced about viruses spread by pigs, and in some cases, these are newly detected viruses. In Malaysia, during the spring of 1999, tens of thousands of pigs were exterminated in order to stop the spread of a virus found in the pig population and transmitted to humans by way of mosquitoes. Other reports have surfaced that pigs are capable of altering certain influenza viruses, such as those found in birds, thus making these mutated viruses able to adversely affect humans. In addition, each cell of a pig contains a retrovirus, for which the long-term effects are unknown.

What About Beef?

For about the last thirty years, rumors about beef tarnished its reputation in some nutrition circles. Greatly undeserved, this fall from nutritional grace was based primarily on the myths about saturated fat. The nutritional content of beef gradually became undervalued because of erroneous assumptions about fat that started to permeate the popular press. No good reason exists to limit beef in your diet. In fact, nutritionally speaking, beef is a powerhouse food.

Beef represents a rich source of B vitamins such as thiamine, riboflavin, niacin, B6, and B12. The latter is found only in animal foods. B12 is needed to carry oxygen to muscles and is also involved in converting food into energy. Some vegetarians consume dairy foods so they might obtain an adequate supply of B12; however, vegetarians who eliminate all dairy foods are invariably deficient in B12, which may lead to anemia.

If you look on the shelves of supermarkets, you will find cereals and flour products that are fortified with vitamin B12—and other vitamins and minerals, too. But if you eat a wide variety of animal protein foods, including beef, there is no need to rely on products fortified with synthetically produced B complex vitamins. Beef contains the form of B12 that the body can use efficiently, so I do not recommend relying on "second hand" sources.

Beef also provides a generous supply of certain essential minerals. For example, heme-iron, a type of iron easily absorbed by the body, occurs in beef but is not available in plant sources of iron. While many foods contain iron, beef remains the best source of the kind of iron the body uses most efficiently.

Those who dismiss the importance of animal protein usually fail to mention the importance of iron for overall health. Iron is of critical importance because the mineral carries oxygen to all your cells, and every cell in the body must have oxygen to function normally. Iron deficiencies eventually lead to anemia, which is characterized by depleted energy and fatigue. Every person needs iron, but pregnant women, growing children, adolescents, and all women during their reproductive years have the greatest need for this mineral. These groups are the most at risk for iron deficiencies. Researchers established decades ago that children with iron deficiencies may not develop normally and are more likely to have difficulties in school. Normal intellectual development is dependent on many things, of course, but the need for iron is well established. Unfortunately, iron deficiencies during pregnancy are common and contribute to the incidence of premature delivery and low birth weight.

In addition to iron, beef supplies generous amounts of zinc, another mineral essential for normal growth and development. Zinc is one of nature's infection fighters because it is critical for optimal immune system functioning.

Is Beef an Antioxidant?

Antioxidants are substances that counteract the effects of unstable molecules called free radicals. Free radicals are involved in the cause of numerous conditions and diseases, such as cancer and diseases affecting arteries and blood vessels. Vitamins C and E are two well-known antioxidant substances. You may not have heard of the fatty acid called *conjugated linoleic acid—CLA*—but it is a potentially important fatty acid and it is found primarily in beef. Animal research results to date show that CLA has the ability to lower LDL (low-density lipoprotein), the so-called "bad" cholesterol, and in general, promote lean body tissue in laboratory animals. Human research among males involved in resistance training showed that supplementation with CLA produced measurable increases in strength. While more research is needed, it is possible that CLA may emerge as one of the "feature attractions" of beef.

Protein Consumption and Longevity

In the summer of 1999, a report appeared in the *New York Times* suggesting that a calorie-restricted diet may prevent some cellular changes commonly associated with aging. Other research has been interpreted to show that restricting calories is the pathway to slowing down the aging process. The reasoning behind these interpretations involves glucose metabolism. When glucose combines with oxygen, the process forms free radicals, which damage cells.

I view these data somewhat differently. I do not believe that calorie restriction is at the heart of the research findings, but rather, points to glucose itself as the key. High carbohydrate diets are by definition high glucose diets, and therefore, have the potential to increase cellular damage, or put another way, hasten damage to the cells.

As I see it, The LifeForce Plan, which is high in protein and relatively low in carbohydrates, results in keeping excessive glucose levels consistently reduced, thereby decreasing the rate of cellular damage caused by free radical formation. In this way, it is a diet that may promote longevity and well being along the way. In addition, when glucose is reduced the body avoids surges in the hormone insulin. Disturbances in glucose and insulin metabolism often lead to diabetes, which is known to shorten life. Your best insurance against diabetes is to consume adequate protein and eat *real* foods while avoiding products that contain little else but white flour, sugar, and hydrogenated vegetable oils.

Test the Information For Yourself

With few exceptions, for most people the best, most *usable* source of protein is animal protein, including beef, game meats, lamb, veal, poultry, eggs, and fish. These are superior protein sources, and are more beneficial to the body than milk proteins. Vegetable protein sources provide amino acids in the diet, but they generally are not consistently reliable sources of the amount of protein the body needs to replace proteins that are broken down on a continuous basis.

My patients do not count protein grams and it is usually not necessary to keep track of exact intake. In general, guidelines call for adults to consume between 60 and 100 grams of *high quality* protein per day. During the early weeks of The LifeForce Plan, the body is undergoing detoxification and protein demands are increased. So, I recommend consuming protein-rich meals, without concern about fat consumption. Virtually all my patients report that this diet immediately leads to increased energy. You will know the plan is working by the way you feel. Certainly, you will need to follow all the other components of the diet, including the water consumption and the sweating. In addition to increased energy, protein consumption will begin triggering a release of fluids from your body's tissues.

In the last part of the twentieth century we lived in an era that devalued fat and in the tradition of "guilt by association," sources of complete protein were devalued, too. However, I believe we are entering a time when the misinformation of the past will be exposed more and more. The LifeForce Plan is firmly planted in principles that promote health, help prevent disease, and may even help you extend the number of years that you enjoy vitality and good health.

6

Staying Healthy in a Toxic World

> Had I not tried it myself, I never would have believed that these dietary changes could create such health and well-being. My joint pain has been gone and I've been free of symptoms for four years.
> —*Michele Moul, D.C.*

Typically, after following the LifeForce Plan for several weeks patients tell me they feel better than they have in years. Sometimes, their renewed energy motivates them to assess their lives, perhaps taking trips they've postponed or creating some new professional and personal goals. While poor health tends to deplete one's "life force," it's equally true that robust health can often lead people to behave as if they have "a new lease on life," as the saying goes. So, now that these patients feel terrific, they ask me how they can *maintain* their health and energy.

Living a healthful life in a toxic and complex world represents one of the biggest challenges we will ever face. Most of us struggle to find the balance between professional and personal demands on our time and we probably want to play hard, too. Meanwhile, amidst a world replete with choices we try to carve out time to rest. In addition, the more we learn about our inevitable exposure to environmental toxins, the more alarmed we become. I've known people, and you probably have, too, who refuse to go to restaurants because they're afraid of toxins in the food. Some people are afraid of walking on their city streets because of the toxic fumes from busses and cars.

All of us face the daunting task of staying mindful of steps we can take to maintain our health without isolating ourselves and becoming so concerned with health hazards that we no longer enjoy a normal life. When fear of the environment robs us of our ability to live fully in the world, the whole point of enjoying good health is defeated. The best solution involves facing environmental realities, learning to do our best to minimize problems, and then getting on with our lives. (In the back of this book, you will find information about buying all the products discussed in this chapter.)

First, the Bad News

The Environmental Protection Agency (EPA) lists at least *50,000 chemicals,* and fewer than 1,000 have been tested for their potential effects on environmental and human health. If you visit the EPA website, you will see that the agency attempts to list new chemicals and it encourages companies to participate in their monitoring process. The EPA, within the confines of its relatively small budget, attempts to quantify the chemicals added to the environment each year, but no practical or effective way exists to get a completely accurate assessment. However, based on current figures, 7.3 *billion* pounds of toxic chemicals were disposed of on- and off-site, and the EPA acknowledges that this represents only a portion of what is being dumped into our environment in this country alone. Without question, when we start to hear about toxic *anything* described in billions, we're likely to be frightened.

We Are Connected to Our Environment

In her important book, *Non-toxic, Natural, and Earth Wise,* Deborah Lynn Bass offers data that demonstrate that we cannot view ourselves as separate from the air or water or any substance that makes its way into the food we eat. For example, our fat cells store toxins, most of which have the ability to bind to fat. According to the National Adipose Tissue Survey, 100 percent of individuals tested positive for certain chemicals, including dioxins. Through considerable effort on the part of scientists and environmentalists, some toxic chemicals have been banned from use in the United

States, but they can still show up in the body long after exposure. As long as they remain in the body's tissues, they are potentially harmful. Toxic chemicals, and the effects of these substances, tend to linger and their damage is difficult to reverse. The key to neutralizing the potential harm involves converting fat soluble toxins into water soluble toxins that can then be excreted from the body. This is what the LifeForce Plan is designed to do.

As you probably have observed, the concept of "detoxification" is relatively new. Just a few decades ago, few people gave much thought to potentially damaging substances in their food and water, let alone going through periodic detoxification processes. Medical discussions about detoxification tended to be reserved for acute episodes of toxicity, such as over-exposure to lead resulting from an environmental accident. Today, however, our job is to address *chronic exposure* to toxins and minimize their impact.

A Different View of Detoxification Cycles

It may sound odd to you, but I don't believe that we "catch" a cold, so much as the body's detoxification process is stimulated or triggered. For example, one person in an office comes to work with what appears to be a bad cold and soon, half the office calls in sick. According to the contagion theory of illness, exposure to bacteria and/or viruses cause us to develop a sore throat, sinus congestion, and the various symptoms we associate with upper respiratory infections. The contagion theory is just that, a theory, and no one can definitively say what causes individuals to develop common upper respiratory illnesses. In fact, in one study, researchers swabbed the nasal passages of a person with a cold and then swabbed nasal passages of 12 other people, thereby exposing them to the bacteria. Only two of the 12 developed a cold, which is a low number, especially when we consider the theory that what we call common colds are highly contagious.

Let's look at another theory. In *Jacobson's Organ,* a recent book by Lyall Watson, the olfactory pathway contains an organ named after Ludwig Levin Jacobson, the scientist who discovered it in the early nineteenth century. Jacobson found that the nasal septum contains two tiny pits, one on each side, which contain several million fringed receptor cells. Odors are also processed in the olfactory bulb, which has pathways to the limbic portion of the brain, often referred to as the emotional or instinctual brain. It appears, however, that Jacobson's organ, which scientists often refer to (probably incorrectly) as an evolutionary remnant, is not specifically involved with detecting and identifying odors, but may be the pathway for other kinds of signals. (The signals may also be processed in the hypothalamus, the part of the brain that controls many basic physiological functions, and the limbic brain.) For example, it is possible that the invisible chemical signals we call pheromones are processed by way of Jacobson's organ.

You may know that pheromones are presumed to influence mating behavior in animals—including humans. It's been documented that women living together in dormitories, or even women working closely in an office, will "synchronize" their menstrual cycles within a few months. Other studies have shown that men will avoid stalls in a restroom where a presumed pheromonal substance has been placed. In other words, invisible substances are at work that, in a sense, mark territory, not out in the jungles and savannas, but in modern restrooms. Pheromones represent one type of chemical signal, but many others may exist.

The presence of Jacobson's organ offers an explanation for the theory that we can trigger a detoxification process that produces cold symptoms in each other. Consider that we shed about 40 million flakes of skin each day and the air is filled with these substances that contain viruses, bacteria, and pheromones, and perhaps other forms of chemical signals, in the air. We may develop cold symptoms because our bodies need to detoxify; your office mate may be just the person whose chemical signals stimulate your congestion and sore throat, which is actually a detoxification process. In other words, cold symptoms result from invisible chemical signals in the air.

Perhaps those who aren't vulnerable to the detox trigger are those who are not already in toxic overload. This also suggests an additional reason to induce sweating on a regular basis. Remember that the skin is a major detoxification organ and if you don't do the sweating regimen on the LifeForce Plan, you will likely develop cold symptoms.

Most of us associate fevers with infections, but scientists still do not know for sure why the body creates a fever. Perhaps the heat generated is intended to induce sweating, which in turn helps fight the infection because it detoxifies the body. In the typical medical model, the fever is something to be "fought" and then taken together, the other symptoms are called a "cold." However, using the holistic model, we may still label the congestion and sore throat a cold, but we treat it differently. In most cases, we would seek to detoxify the body and avoid antibiotics as an all-purpose solution. The explanation for common cold symptoms may be far simpler, and the key may be clearing toxins from the body.

Detoxification and the Liver

It bears repeating that the liver is the body's key detoxification organ, and the diet I developed concentrates on helping the liver do its job better. The liver acts as a kind of "brain" or "communication center" within the body in that it interacts with other organs. The liver can become overburdened, not only with the chemicals we ingest, but also with cellular waste products. When this happens, our ability to stay healthy within the chemical soup of our environment is compromised. I could have called The LifeForce Plan the "liver detoxification plan" because of its ability to decrease the toxic load on the liver. I believe the diet leads to a dramatic improvement of a variety of symptoms because of improved liver function, which in turn improves the function of all detoxification pathways in the body.

Our challenge is to maintain improved liver function through several steps or measures, but without driving ourselves into a frenzy over issues we cannot control. In other words, we may not be able to change the world, but we can address our nutritional needs and alter our home environment with a few relatively minor initiatives.

Good Food/Bad Food?

I often hesitate to recommend only organic food, but not because I don't believe it's superior to the produce you find in your standard supermarkets. However, I don't like to see the kind of stress that people put on themselves in order to find what they think of as "pure" food. I would rather see you use some basic commonsense principles and follow some simple practices. Create most of your diet from the allowed foods on the LifeForce Plan and use carbohydrate foods, such as breads and beans and sweets in moderation.

As I've said earlier, you should avoid pork because it carries viruses. I also recommend limiting oranges in your diet. The skin of the fruit contains so much fungus it can release spores into the air in your house. Oranges increase mucous production in the body, and these cells end up in the lymphatic system and create congestion, thereby compromising the body's detoxification pathways. (Tangerines are not affected in the same way, however, so you can include them with all the other fruits.) Lymphatic congestion also interferes with nutrient absorption. Most nuts and dried fruits have fungus associated with them, so eat them in moderation. I believe almonds and pine nuts are the best of the commonly available nuts.

Patients often ask me about dairy foods, and many people do not feel well after eating cheese or ice cream or yogurt because they have developed an allergy to dairy products. This may result from years of consuming dairy products that have been saturated with pesticides used in the animal feed. These chemicals, along with cattle vaccines and bovine growth hormone, make their way into the milk and the variety of dairy foods produced from it.

While lactose intolerance certainly is an issue, I think many people may not have an allergy to dairy as such, but rather, are reacting to the chemicals in the products. A learned allergic response to dairy exists, but the body can release a dairy allergy. The LifeForce Plan is a step in changing the body's response to dairy foods. In my own case, it took a year after completing the LifeForce Plan for my body to alter its response to dairy foods, and I used only organic products, meaning dairy foods made from milk from cows that had not been fed pesticides, bovine growth hormone, and so forth. You may find that your body reacts in a similar way.

Your Health Starts with Digestion

Millions of people take daily doses of vitamins, mostly because they want a nutritional "insurance policy." However, unless these nutrients are absorbed they have no effect at all, so many of these nutritional supplements and the dollars spent buying them are wasted because the body cannot use them. The digestive system is the body's health maintenance gatekeeper, and a healthy balance of natural intestinal flora is essential to use the nutrients in food and supplements.

The diet in the LifeForce Plan allows different parts of the body to heal, particularly the colon, an important organ for eliminating toxins. In restoring digestive health, you will also reverse or prevent digestive conditions such as constipation, which I believe is linked with liver function. Accumulation of toxins causes the muscular layers of the colon walls to break down, which then leads to constipation. If you are not having two to three bowel movements each day, you should address your digestive health.

The LifeForce Plan may take care of any constipation problems because it eliminates the toxic overload on the liver. However, some people also require a colon-cleansing program. One of the products I recommend is Colon Program, produced by Eden's Secrets.

A company named Peterson's Health also produces intestinal cleansing products: Sonne's #7 is formulated with bentonite clay and absorbs and draw toxins, such as bacteria and viruses off the intestinal wall; Sonne's #9 is made with psyllium powder (a fibrous substance) that gently scrapes and cleanses the intestinal tracts. These products include directions for their use. Both Eden's Secret and Peterson's Health have been around for many years and they are ethical companies with quality products.

A colon-cleansing program is a measure to undertake periodically, not as a daily event. Such a program is meant to restore regularity by eliminating accumulated toxins. However, you can take other steps on a regular, even daily basis to promote a healthy colon and intestinal tract. Acidophilus supplements can help maintain the right flora balance in the colon and large intestine, which optimizes absorption of nutrients from food and supplements. In addition, acidophilus helps the body synthesize B vitamins, and makes vitamins from foods and supplements more useful.

Flora Prime is manufactured specifically for the LifeForce Plan. After researching and trying many formulas over a 13 year period, I decided to combine the best of what's available into one product. Two additional companies, Jarrow Formulas and Klaire Labs, also produce quality acidophilus products.

In addition to acidophilus, digestive enzymes can help the body break down the foods you consume and enhance absorption, thus optimizing the nutritional value of your meals. Most health food stores carry digestive enzyme supplements to take before eating.

Most of these products are adequate, but if you want the top of the line, I recommend enzymes produced by Transformation Enzyme Corporation, based in Houston, Texas.

The Supplement Maze

If your digestive system doesn't work well, which is the case when candidiasis is present, taking handfuls of vitamin supplements is not going to do much good, which is one of the reasons I recommend taking acidophilus and digestive enzymes. In addition, if you're taking a multivitamin as a nutritional supplement to prevent deficiencies, then you should take it with a meal. In general, water-soluble vitamins, such as the B complex vitamins, should be consumed with foods. However, if you're using certain nutrients therapeutically, then it's sometimes best to take them away from food. For example, vitamin E in a dose high enough to be used therapeutically can be taken between meals.

The nutritional supplement industry is big business and, to date, we don't have good quality control. Quality varies among companies, but overall, I believe Country Life and New Chapter vitamins produce consistently high quality products, including multivitamin supplements. Thorne Research produces a very high quality hypoallergenic line of supplements. Like multivitamin supplements, vitamin B complex products are plentiful; yet, an effective B complex vitamin is rare. I prefer the B complex produced by Thorne Research.

Detox Essentials is an important feature of The LifeForce Plan and because it is an important antioxidant substance you should continue taking it (1 to 2 capsules a day) even after you are finished with the LifeForce Plan. Detox Essentials contains Ester-C, which is the most easily absorbed vitamin C available. This innovative Ester-C product is combined with Red Clover and Echinacea, both of which help to purify the blood and lymphatic system. Other companies make ester C products, but after making comparisons, I still believe Detox Essentials is the superior choice.

It is difficult to find a good vitamin E supplement because many are synthetic formulations that are of little value. Dry vitamin E packaged in a capsule is not an effective product, no matter who produces them. The A.C. Grace Company produces Unique E, which I give to my patients and use myself. Vitamin E is not stored in the body, and while it isn't necessary to take it every day, its preventive effect is gone in two or three days. Along with acidophilus and vitamin C, vitamin E is an important supplement to take on a regular basis.

As with vitamin E, it's not easy to find a good vitamin A supplement. After researching many brands, I recommend a carotene complex supplement produced by Country Life. You have probably heard that *beta*carotene is beneficial, but Country Life's product contains other carotenes as well. Carotenes are not just one substance, but a family of nutrients, which together are valuable immune system stimulants.

Because of increased media attention focused on osteoporosis, calcium is much in the news these days; however, not all calcium supplements are created equal. Klaire Labs, a good producer of acidophilus, also makes Cal-Assimilate Plus, a calcium supplement, and Multi-Mineral Complex, a multi-mineral supplement. Country Life and Jarrow also produce good calcium supplements. When you choose a calcium product, make sure it is formulated from hydroxyaptite calcium, which provides an acid base that increases absorption. Calcium carbonate, the type of calcium found in Tums, is used because it is inexpensive and, of course, the products cost less than Cal-Assimilate Plus or a Country Life product. However, ineffective calcium supplements are not a bargain at any price.

Glutathione is an amino acid residue that has many useful functions in the body. It is synthesized inside the cells, but no good precursor exists in the body's tissues. However, a product called Immunocal, produced by Immunotech Research, helps the body produce glutathione. I recommend Immunocal in many different situations, and it is especially useful for men and women who engage in high-intensity workouts, such as running marathons, because it helps the body handle high oxidative stress. It is also valuable in the treatment of a variety of degenerative diseases. I've recommended it to patients with Parkinson's disease, Alzheimer's disease, cataracts, malnutrition, AIDS, and cancer. I have noted that in some instances, Immunocal has helped prevent cancer in one site from entering the lymphatic system, which is the pathway that cancer spreads to other distant sitcs throughout the body.

Using Herbal Products Effectively

Herbal products present concerns similar to those I raised about vitamin supplements. While some within the industry are looking at the quality of production standards, some issues remain unresolved. For example, considerable variation exists in the time it takes from harvesting the herbs to complete processing and packaging them. An herbal product that has been sitting in storage or on health food store shelves may lose potency and be rendered ineffective.

Renee Ponder, owner of Herbal Magic, started her company because she found that mass produced herbal products tend not to work. She decided to produce and market her own line of products, which do not sit in warehouses and lose their effectiveness. Herbal Magic formulas are more costly than the off-the-shelf products you find in supermarkets and typical pharmacies, but while higher cost doesn't always guarantee a better product, you can be fairly certain that inexpensive, mass produced herbals are not high quality.

Most consumers must rely on expert help to choose the best herbal formulas. My patients can trust what I recommend because I've spent so much time researching the vast array of available herbal preparations. If a healthcare provider recommends specific nutritional supplements or herbal formulations, find out why he or she believes they are superior to other available products.

Additional Recommendations

Nutritional products tend to come and go and sometimes a trend becomes a fad that is gone within a few years. Every now and then, however, new products fill a need and continue to make inroads into the nutritional markets. A company called Essentially Yours has a preparation called Calorad, which is marketed as a weight loss product in the U.S, although I do not believe that is necessarily the best reason to use it. In essence, Calorad is a collagen-based liquid formula, in which collagen (an important type of protein) is broken down, purified, and reformulated in such a way that the amino acids retained in the formula work with the body's growth hormone, thus enabling the body to burn fat and manufacture collagen. For this reason, it is promoted as an aid to weight loss.

Based on my experience with detoxification, the body does not necessarily burn fat if the fatty tissue is holding—harboring—toxins. Remember that this is a protective mechanism, because if you burn the fat, the toxins will release into the body. In order to prevent this flood of toxins, the body will burn protein tissue instead. However, if you detoxify with The LifeForce Plan, you can then safely take Calorad and encourage the body to burn fat. Patients who have stubborn excess pounds often find that the body will burn fat once toxins have been safely eliminated from the body.

As we age, the body replaces muscle tissue with fat, but Calorad may burn away these fatty accumulations and rebuild the body from the inside out. On several occasions I've felt these fatty deposits as bumps when I've examined patients. After using Calorad, these fatty infiltrations disappeared. I have also observed that Calorad helps improve the skin and minimizes wrinkles. It appears this product has a number of uses.

Essentially Yours also produces Agrisept-L, a supplement made from the seeds of tangerines, grapefruits, limes, and lemons. Agrisept-L has antiviral and antibiotic properties, and I also recommend it because of its anti-parasitic effects. Eliminating or controlling the presence of parasites in the body is one of the functions of the liver. When the liver is overwhelmed, then parasites increase, and Agrisept-L can help eliminate them by creating an unfavorable environment. When I recommend this product to patients, I generally tell them to take 10-25 drops, 2-3 times a day. They can mix the product with water, or if they prefer, with a small amount of juice, assuming they've completed the LifeForce Plan.

Sometimes patients will accuse me of being against house pets because I describe them as reservoirs for parasites. But I'm not against enjoying pets; I just want my patients to understand that animals carry parasites. This is why I recommend that patients give Agrisept-L to their pets, in dosages appropriate for animals. For example, give your cat one to three drops per day in a bowl of fresh water. I've seen cats cured of feline leukemia when treated with Agrisept-L.

Protecting your pets from parasites helps protect your health, too, because you can contract parasites from your pets. Parasites are not necessarily worms you can see, but rather are microscopic and can travel in the air from feces in the litter box to you. You can also pick up parasites from kissing your dogs and cats. So, love your pets, but protect them from parasites and make them safer for the whole family to be around.

As concerns about the overuse of antibiotics continue, products like Agrisept-L that protect against infection will become increasingly popular. Royal jelly is an another substance with special value for fighting infections, particularly upper respiratory infections, colds, and flu. I recommend Premiere One Royal Jelly, which is formulated in a base of honey, a powerful natural antibiotic. I recommend purchasing the 30-milligram concentration of Premier One Royal Jelly.

Honey products are generally not recommended for children under age two. However, I've never seen any adverse reactions from giving Premiere One Royal Jelly to these young children. In fact, I've seen it cure colds and flu that medications couldn't touch. The product is easy to give to children, too, because they love the taste.

As an aside, I spend considerable time researching products. Essentially Yours, which distributes Agrisept-L and Calorad is a multilevel company, but you can visit their website and sign up as a distributor, which means that you buy the products at a discount. You are under no obligation to sell the product and become part of the marketing network, which is what puts some people off about these companies.

Your Home Is Your Haven

Ideally, our homes are healing places, pleasant havens where we tend to ourselves—mind, body, and spirit—and in which we relax and renew our energy. I hope you will think about your home environment, not only in terms of chemicals and potential toxicity, but also its emotional or psychological atmosphere. It makes no sense to concentrate all our efforts on purifying our air and water and eating healthful meals, for example, while we still work to excess, leave our relationships untended, or deprive ourselves of needed rest and sleep.

That said, I offer the following ideas to improve your physical environment:

Air and Water Quality:

Pure water is an essential component in any health improvement program, yet we often take it for granted. Water is a universal solvent. It dissolves almost anything. Research has shown that water holds an energy imprint of almost everything that passes through it, even after the substance is no longer present. The "information" in the water can be communicated from one body of water to another, even over long distances and separation. All living organisms are influenced by the quality of water in their environments.

Modern water processing prevents the normal flow of water in our streams and rivers, which inhibits the natural revitalization of water supplies. In addition, chlorine, ammonia, fluoride, and heavy metals such as aluminum, poison our water and rob it of its vitality. We drink this water and bathe in it and over time, we risk depressing our already over-taxed immune systems, thus disrupting normal cell environment. Heating water in a microwave further adversely affects the quality of the water and compromises our ability to maintain or restore health.

I recommend that you take steps to improve air and water quality within your home. Look into products available through Fred Van Liew's Essential Water and Air Company, which uses modern technologies in their home filtering systems. Reverse osmosis technology combined with sediment, carbon or carbon/KDF and carbon block technologies represent the optimal systems to produce water purity. For example, this company developed an excellent shower filter that helps reduce your exposure to chlorine. When you step into your steaming shower you create a chamber in which the mixture of water and air creates a situation in which chemicals are released in gas form. Most of us enjoy hot showers, but the hotter the water, the more efficiently the gases are released. We inhale these chemicals and they are absorbed through our skin.

Most other water filtering act either by a reverse osmosis process or by a carbon blocking process. Since Fred's systems include both, his systems are the most comprehensive and beneficial available at this time. I recommend using a *central* water purification process when possible rather than a system that purifies only drinking water in a pitcher filter or attached to the faucet. These systems remove only chlorine and chlorine by-products and chemicals. Fluoride and heavy metals and other substances are allowed to pass through. Thus, to maximize benefits, all the water used in your household should be filtered

Fluoride content in water is a significant issue. Fluoride is added to water in many parts of the world and most commercial toothpaste products add fluoride, too. Although well intended, the disadvantages of adding fluoride to drinking water and other products outweigh any perceived benefits (i.e., preventing tooth decay). Fluoride depresses thyroid activity, causes premature aging in the body, and adversely influences synthesis of collagen in the bone, tendons, muscles, cartilage, skin, lungs, and kidneys. Some suggest that fluoride promotes development of bone cancer, and it may have a disruptive effect on various body tissues and increase tumor growth in cancer-prone individuals. For this reason, purifying your water and neutralizing both chlorine and fluoride represent steps you can take to improve the quality of your home environment.

For fluoride-free dental care products, I recommend toothpaste and mouthwashes made by Desert Essence. (Desert Essence also makes aluminum-free deodorants.) Another company that has been around a long time, Tom's of Maine, produces personal care products, including both fluoridated and non-fluoridated toothpaste, as well as a line of mouthwashes.

To improve air quality, I use a combination of ozone and an ion generator in my home. The extra oxygen molecule in ozone helps bind particles in the air, thus helping to neutralize the effects of various toxic substances and things like dust mites. Ion generators achieve an additional benefit. You may have heard some people talk about a connection between pain in their joints or a developing headache and a weather front that's on the way. This isn't just a folk belief. Waves of *positive* ions do indeed precede a weather front, which in some people trigger joint pain or allergy symptoms. Negative ion generators can balance the positive ions in the body. These generators and ozone can be used to clear out the house, but you do not necessarily need to use them all the time. Fred Van Liew's Essential Water and Air Company carries these products, as does a company called Living Air. In general, I recommend any kind of filter that cleanses the air in your home.

Travel presents challenges, of course, and you don't have many options when it comes to air quality. However, if you take long car trips for work or pleasure, I recommend using distilled water. While consuming only distilled water over a period of time may lead to mineral depletion in the body, it is probably the safest water when you're on the road. If you are traveling for long periods and water quality is a concern, you can improve distilled water by adding liquid trace minerals to distilled water.

Radiation Exposure:

Reluctantly, I have come to believe that our gene pool is being weakened, and our grandparents and great-grandparents were more resistant to disease and degenerative diseases, primarily because they experienced less exposure to environmental toxins, including radiation. We usually look at the past and marvel at how our ancestors survived such harsh conditions and uncertainty about basic needs, such as a reliable food supply. Their time on the planet seemed more perilous than our stay here, at least on a day-to-day basis, but ironically, they may have been *constitutionally* stronger than we are today. From birth, virtually every person on the planet is exposed to electromagnetic radiation. When we add radiation exposure to the weakening effects of environmental toxins, antibiotics, and vaccinations, we gradually reduce the body's natural resistance and curative abilities.

Remember, too, that the body generates its own electrical activity. Of the organs in our body, the brain first, and the heart second, generate the most electrical activity, and their function is influenced by the electromagnetic field. Too many of us spend hours and hours in front of computer screens and we work in environments where we are constantly exposed to electromagnetic fields. We must make the effort to neutralize the radiation exposure by carefully selecting low-radiation computer screens, for example, or by using a protective screen that helps reduce exposure to the electromagnetic field the screens generate.

You may have heard reports recommending that the common clock radios many of us have on our nightstands constitute a nightly exposure to an electromagnetic field next to your head. Clarus Products International, based in Bellevue, Washington, sells products, such as clocks and watches, that neutralize electromagnetic radiation. In the future, we are likely to see more products and companies emerge to help reduce radiation exposure and damage.

Choosing Safe Personal Care and Household Products

You can increase your peace of mind if you pay attention to the common household and personal products you use every day. For example, the popular grocery store soaps and detergents and shampoos contain perfuming agents and other chemicals. Perfumed products, such as dish soap, leave residues behind on your dishes and tableware. The perfume used in soaps and shampoos and the vast array of scents and colognes you use on your body remain present in the air and these substances shut down lymphatic pathways. While scented cosmetic products are firmly entrenched in modern cultural life, I recommend using them on a limited basis. I also suggest that you use low-phosphate laundry detergents, which are safer for the environment and do not leave residue on your clothing.

Choose deodorant and antiperspirant products carefully. The underarm area is an important region for the lymph system and deodorant powders or gels generally cover several inches of the area and block the lymphatic pathways. In addition, these products generally contain aluminum derivatives and evidence exists that aluminum can cross the blood brain barrier, meaning that traces of the metal can migrate to the brain. Although all the causes remain unknown, aluminum has been linked to the development of Alzheimer's disease. Desert Essence produces a line of safe deodorant products.

The Five Star Soap Company produces pure soaps with high-grade vegetable tallow and pure butter oils. Their products, including their shampoos, contain no perfumes or dyes. This company also makes a very good line of laundry and dishwasher detergents.

When it comes to hair care, most shampoos sold today have harsh, damaging detergents that create mounds of lather, but place severe stress on the hair follicles, glands, and scalp. Common chemicals in these products can cause damage to the scalp and glands, while stripping away essential nutrients and oils. A company called Organic Excellence offers shampoos and conditioners made without alcohol, propylene glycol, artificial scents and colors, harsh detergents like sodium laurel sulfate, olefin, sulfonate, myreth sulfate, or any derivative of lauryl alcohol. Organic Excellence products help to create a healthy environment to support the natural uninterrupted cycle of hair growth and replacement. Another good shampoo is Soignee, which I have used for years, and continue to do so.

Too Tired to Sleep?

Odd as it sounds, you need energy to go to sleep. Sometimes you cross a threshold where you are too tired to sleep—that isn't just your imagination. I've found that on the occasions this has happened to me, drinking a cup of coffee helps me fall asleep. This may seem like a contradiction, but I don't believe it is. The boost of energy was enough to allow me to sleep. According to traditional Chinese medical thinking, your major detoxification organs operate while you sleep. This is what the detoxification "schedule" looks like: 11:00 pm-1:00 am, gallbladder; 1:00 am-3:00 am, liver; 3:00-5:00 am, lung; and, 5:00-7:00, large intestine.

You need energy for these organs to work while you sleep. As you can see from the schedule above, the major organs—liver, lung, and large intestine—are working at their peak while you sleep. When patients tell me they wake up in the middle of the night, the majority of them tell me this happens about 3:00 am. This probably happens because when you're switching from liver detoxification to lung detoxification your system is in "high gear" and the demand for energy is great. When people are awake between 3:00 and 5:00, this usually indicates that they do not have enough energy to stay asleep. If this happens to you, this means that you need to rest, and when you slow down your life and get the rest you need, your sleep patterns are likely to improve.

This and That

Over the years I've noted various things that may be helpful to you as you improve the quality of your life. For example, sweating baths are an essential part of The LifeForce Plan, and I urge my patients to continue them after they're finished with the plan. Hot baths and saunas come to us from many places in Europe and are part of traditional health care wisdom. We need to renew these practices because they have great value for our health. I recommend taking three or four sweating baths or sessions in the sauna each week. If you groan over this recommendation and protest that you don't have the time, consider what that says about the pace of your life. The skin is a major detoxification organ and sweating is an efficient detoxification method. Make time to relax in a hot bath or sauna.

No matter how much we try to avoid it, most of us become ill now and then. Food poisoning afflicts most of us from time to time, and I have found that Coca-Cola, yes, the common soft drink, is one of the best ways to cure it quickly. Classic Coke is the best soft drink choice. (Almost everyone is surprised to hear me say that.) Other health care providers have noticed that Coke can settle upset stomachs and Coke syrup is actually an old home remedy that we should probably revive.

In general, I do not oppose consuming coffee and tea with caffeine in your diet. I don't exclude them from the LifeForce Plan because they do not feed the candida. However, caffeine can overwork the adrenals, and just like stress, the stimulant can deplete the ability of these "stress management" glands to do their work. We live in a stressful society and when we consume caffeine, we may add to the stress load on the body.

Alcohol overworks the liver and tends to interfere with its detoxification job. This is not to say that you should never touch alcohol, but if you consume excessive amounts of alcoholic drinks, then it will be essentially impossible to maintain optimal health in large part because of poor liver function.

Enjoy Your Health—and Your Life

I recommend that you experiment with the home care products and personal items discussed in this chapter. As much as you can, try to stay current about environmentally safe products, along with developments in healthcare that do not rely on antibiotics and synthetic drugs. Maintain healthy skepticism about the so-called miracle drugs that offer a quick fix for health problems.

Meanwhile, create a lifestyle that supports your health: balance your work with play and nurture yourself and those you love in a home that is a true refuge. Most of all realize that although you live in a toxic world, it does no good to hide in your house, isolated and lonely. Open the windows, let in the light, both figuratively and literally. Do what you can to protect yourself and then live fully with energy and spirit.

7

Answers to Your Questions

Choose which seems best and, in the doing,
it will become agreeable and easy.
—*Pythagoras (about 550 B.C.)*

Over the years, I've found that some questions about the LifeForce Plan come up again and again. For many people, this plan is very different from other dietary guidelines or detoxification programs they have heard about or tried, and I often think that some patients can't quite believe that the LifeForce Plan really is as simple as it sounds! Other people attempt to take shortcuts or leave out components and they need clarification about the importance of each step. I assembled the most frequently asked questions in this chapter, and I trust they address issues of interest to you.

1. **I travel a great deal, so how can I adhere to the plan when I must eat in restaurants?**
   The LifeForce Plan is quite easy to follow when you are "on the road," because it includes real—and common—food. Most restaurant menus list the kinds of foods you can have, from vegetable omelets and fresh fruit to mixed green salads to grilled fish and steamed brown rice. Ask for lemon wedges and plain olive oil if you want dressing on a salad. If you find yourself in a sea of fast food restaurants along a highway, you can always settle for a hamburger without the bun and many of these restaurants have salads, too. While I recommend only certain

types of oil, I do not want patients to panic if they find out that some canola or safflower oil or other types of oil has slipped into a dish they order in a restaurant. Avoid bread, pasta, grains, dairy, and sweets, and focus on the wide range of food you can have, even in restaurants or when you travel.

2. **Are artificial sweeteners, or the newer product, stevia, allowed on the plan? And what about dairy substitutes, such as soymilk?**
   Artificial sweeteners and stevia create the same effect in the body as sugar, in that the body is, in a sense, fooled. The body reacts to the presence of sugar, which often interferes with blood sugar and insulin responses and creates imbalance. Rice or soymilk are also not included because the body responds reflexively to these substances, as if they were the "real thing." Through trial and error, I have found that limiting beverages to water, herb tea, and coffee works best.

3. **Can I eat corn and green peas as vegetables?**
   Both corn and green peas are allowed. Whole corn served as a vegetable is not the same as corn meal, and the body reacts to green peas as a vegetable, even though it is a legume. Other legumes are not allowed because they are difficult for the body to break down and digest.

4. **Can I make vegetable juice or fruit dishes like applesauce?**
   Virtually all fruit juice is a concentrated source of sugar and fruit juices are not on the diet because of their sugar content. Vegetables, with the exception of those with very low sugar content, such as celery, also become concentrated liquid sugar when turned into juice—it takes many carrots, tomatoes, or beets to produce a glass of juice. In general, vegetable juices are not included in the diet, but I suppose if a patient asked me about making celery juice in a juicer at home, it would be acceptable because of the low sugar content. Applesauce is okay if you make it yourself and do not add sweeteners of any kind. However, apple juice is not allowed on the LifeForce Plan.

5. **Why are products such as vinegar or soy sauce not allowed?**
   Vinegar and soy sauce create an environment in the tissues that

affect the acid/alkaline balance in the body and, in addition, the environment is "friendly" to fungus cells, which defeats the purpose of the LifeForce Plan. In general, the foods that are temporarily eliminated from the diet either promote the growth of fungus or they tend to produce allergic reactions. Vinegar, wheat, and dairy are examples of such foods.

6. Is the LifeForce Plan appropriate under special circumstances such as pregnancy or during childhood?
Several women have restored their fertility as they reversed longstanding health problems by using the LifeForce Plan, and these women enjoyed trouble-free pregnancies. The basic diet is actually beneficial for pregnancy because it provides adequate protein and all nutrients the body needs. However, as a precaution, *pregnant women should consult with their doctor before taking Candida Force or any other supplement, herb, or medication.* To date, however, there has never been a problem with Candida Force. I recommend that women use the plan and eliminate their health problems prior to becoming pregnant. In my experience the diet is safe for children in most circumstances. Over the years, several children have been on the diet, one as young as four. Overall, children have far fewer mental barriers to the diet. Adults are quick to raise all their preconceived reasons why they can't start the diet: the time is wrong, they can't fuss with special lunches at work, they don't like to take pills, no time to sweat, and on and on. Kids tend to adjust quickly if parents educate them about the reasons they need to eat certain foods and avoid others. Of course, they may ask when they can eat sweets again, but as a friend of mine said, "The foods they like will still be on the planet when the diet is over." Parents and children often find that it is best to do the diet during the summer when they do not have to cope with school cafeteria food and vending machines.

7. Can I take medications while on the diet?
Do not stop taking any medications on your own, without appropriate advice from your healthcare provider. Many patients are able to eliminate certain medications or cut the dosage after they have completed the plan because various symptoms and

health complaints have disappeared. The diet tends to help the body function more efficiently and the body absorbs and uses nutrients from foods more effectively; this also applies to medications. In addition, the diet leads to improvement in your body's detoxification processes and patients often report fewer and less severe side effects from medications. Ideally, your primary healthcare provider will note that prior health problems are alleviated and, therefore, medications are unnecessary and, eventually, the bottles of prescription medications that have become a part of your life become a thing of the past. I have seen this transformation take place many times.

8. What is the best time to start the diet? Sometimes it seems that there is no good time because I'm always under so much stress.
There will never be a perfect time to start the LifeForce Plan. I believe that virtually everyone can benefit from the diet, which reverses the symptoms caused by systemic candida and restores the body's ability to handle the stress of toxins in the environment and the normal stresses of modern life. Candidiasis causes physical and emotional symptoms and, as you detoxify your body, you will restore emotional equilibrium and improve your ability to cope with everyday stress. The sooner you begin, the sooner you will feel better and the more enjoyable life will be. There will always be weddings and funerals, job interviews, stress at work, vacations, birthdays, holidays, and so forth. With the exception of exotic foreign travel, a situation that may well limit your food choices, do not wait for some ideal month to begin. Start now and within days you will begin feeling better physically and emotionally. As a result, you will be better able to handle the stress that does come along.

9. The Candida Force makes me feel nauseous. Is there something wrong with me? Should I take another product?
I have noticed that some individuals have such severe candidiasis that the die-off reaction is quite severe. In these individuals the elimination pathways are so depressed that they are unable to efficiently clear toxins. In these cases, we simply cut back to 10 or 12 capsules per day to begin and gradually increase the amount as the body adjusts and the nausea goes

away. There is no substitute for Candida Force. I have found that other anti-fungal medications, such as nystatin and nizoral tend to be toxic to the liver and can be taken safely only for a limited period of time. For this reason, I do not recommend any other anti-fungal product other than Candida Force.

10. Can I continue taking nutritional supplements while I am on the LifeForce Diet?

Many patients who come to me are taking numerous supplements, but they may not be of any particular benefit because in the presence of candida the digestive system tends to be inefficient. So, for many people, these expensive supplements are just passing through the digestive system but the nutrients are not absorbed. While they aren't harmful, they aren't particularly helpful either. Chapter 6 contains a list of supplement lines and other products I have found valuable in my practice.

11. Are there any conditions that can be harmed by the LifeForce Plan or which may make the plan ineffective?

In general, no condition renders the plan unsafe and most individuals find that it quickly begins to restore their vitality. However, I have had a few patients who came to me after they had undergone radiation treatments and chemotherapy for cancer. These individuals were so depleted and underweight that they needed to gain some weight before they went on the plan, but most people in this kind of situation do very well on the diet and regain their strength more quickly than they (and often their physicians) thought possible.

12. Is the plan appropriate if I need to gain weight?

I have found that even if patients are already thin and lose a few pounds on the diet, they still feel better. Remember that water in the tissues tends to buffer toxins and the weight that is lost in a thin person is excess fluid, not muscle or body fat. These individuals gain all the benefits of the plan and will feel and look better, regardless of weight loss. If they try to gain the weight back by consuming large quantities of carbohydrate foods, they end up feeling sluggish again. Most of us have preconceived ideas about what we should weigh, but our goal should always be a well-functioning body, regardless of the exact number on the scale.

13. What if I need to lose more weight after the plan is over? Can I stay with the basic eight-week plan until my excess weight is gone?

Although you do not continue taking the Candida Force when the diet is over, you can use the basic plan indefinitely. Some people complain that although they feel better they have not lost unwanted weight. When this occurs, it is generally because these patients tend to be quite toxic and the detoxification process progresses more slowly. As health is restored, which is the purpose of the plan, the body generally adjusts and the excess weight is lost down the road. I know it is difficult to keep from fretting about weight, but I hope you will put your focus on rebuilding your health.

14. Do you recommend strenuous exercise as part of the plan?

As we all know, exercise is good for body, mind, and spirit. Of course I want my patients to engage in some form of exercise. However, I do not prescribe it, because many people come to me with so many health complaints that the first priority is completing the steps of the LifeForce Plan. Exercise does not necessarily enhance the detoxification process and as I have explained, sweating associated with exercise is not the same as sweating in a sauna or a hot bath. Many people attempt to substitute exercise for the hot baths or sauna and soon complain of cold and flu symptoms. My patients usually become more active when they feel better, and because virtually every healthcare professional believes that exercise is part of a healthful lifestyle, almost all my patients eventually make some form of exercise a part of their lives. When you choose an exercise activity, make sure it is something you enjoy. As you probably know, good intentions are not enough to keep you involved in an exercise program you dislike or that is just too dull to keep you motivated.

15. Shortly after starting the diet, my menstrual cycle was heavy and appeared to contain tissue. Why did this happen?

This question comes up often. The menstrual cycle changes because the body is flushing out toxins and, in the process, dead tissue that is bound to the uterine wall is sloughed off. Women may be surprised when this happens, but it is a temporary situation. Look at it as a part of the process of ridding the body of endometrial build-up that serves no useful purpose. It is a natural part of the detoxification process.

16. How often should I repeat the diet?

The LifeForce Plan is designed as a one-time therapy for candidiasis. However, it is a healthful way to eat, and even though you may add your favorite grains or beans or dairy products back to your diet, I recommend that you periodically revisit the diet to get the beneficial effects. I also recommend that you take what you have learned from the diet and continue to use it to maintain health. I periodically go back to the plan as a detoxification program and find that it keeps me in tune with a way of eating—and living—that promotes my well-being. I believe you will find this to be true for you as well.

17. What if I cheat? Will I reverse my progress?

Many people try to find ways around the plan or they look for ways to do the program other than as it's written. Going on and off the diet tends to make the body's detoxification system inefficient because there is a yo-yo effect: a short period of clearing toxins followed by a short period of feeding the fungus with carbohydrates. When we "cheat" at anything, there is conscious intention behind it. This is much different from *inadvertently* consuming an ingredient in a food in a restaurant or in a friend's home. Patients who have stretched the boundaries and have decided to have a glass of wine or some other food have told me they became nauseated or experienced some other rebound effect. The LifeForce Plan is a result of many years of studying what works and what doesn't and there is little room for variation. When it comes to cheating my best advice is: *Don't do it. Invest in yourself and give the plan a chance to change your life.*

8

Enhance Your Meals With Favorite LifeForce Recipes

> I'm eating better than ever in my life. I'm eating
> meat again—it was "forbidden" food. This is a
> powerful plan for me.
>
> —*Bea Young, a patient*

The LifeForce Plan does not have to be dull, but it can be quite easy. Some patients enjoy cooking and use the diet as a chance to experiment and be creative. I include some of their recipes here for your convenience. Many of my patients, and I include myself in this category, prefer to keep the diet very simple. I offer simple suggestions for easy and quick meals. I've also included a section that describes a typical day for me when I'm on the plan. Enjoy this information. Experiment with food and recipes, and if you'd like to share them, send them to me at the LifeForce Center (information listed in the back).

While these recipes are valuable, you can also start your day with a hamburger patty and brown rice or a potato. Make a spinach (or other vegetable) omelet—using more egg whites than yolks. Broil a steak or bake a piece of fish for lunch or dinner. Serve it with any of the dozens of allowed vegetables. Use a variety of foods to make a simple vegetable or chicken soup or a beef or lamb stew. If you're stuck traveling or eating with friends in a fast food restaurant, order a burger and salad for lunch and remove the bun and hold the dressing. This diet is very easy, as you will soon see. If you want to "dress it up" a little, try some of these recipes.

Keeping it Simple Salad Dressings

Commercial dressings contain ingredients not included in the plan, so you must make your own salad dressings. For green salads, I recommend drizzling oil (olive, apricot, or almond) on your salad vegetables, followed by lemon juice. You can add diced tomatoes and herbs if you wish.

One of my patients sent the following recipes for LifeForce Plan mayonnaise, so you can enjoy tuna or chicken salad or slaw.

BLENDER MAYONNAISE 1

2 eggs at room temperature
2 Tbsp. fresh lemon juice
1/2 tsp. salt
1/4 cup oil

Combine eggs, lemon juice, and salt in a blender and blend at high speed for 1 minute. Slowly add the oil until the ingredients are mixed and have thickened. Refrigerate in a glass jar. Use as you would any other mayonnaise.

BLENDER MAYONNAISE 2

2 egg yolks at room temperature
1/2 tsp. sea salt
1 tsp. dry mustard
3 Tbsp. lemon juice
1/4 cup olive oil

Put all ingredients except oil in the food processor or blender. Mix for a few seconds until well blended. Turn off the blender and scrape the sides with a spatula. With the blender or processor running, add the oil in a thin stream. Blend until thick. Makes about one cup. Refrigerate between uses.

If you like pineapple, try the following slaw:

PINEAPPLE SLAW

Combine crushed or finely chopped and drained pineapple with finely grated cabbage. (Vary amounts to suit your needs.) Add blender mayonnaise to taste. You can add carrots and other vegetables to add variety.

EGG AND SPINACH BAKE

Chopped, fresh spinach (enough to fill a quart casserole dish)
1 egg, beaten until fluffy.

Heat your oven to 350 degrees, and oil the casserole dish. Mix the spinach and egg and pour into the dish. Bake for 30 minutes. Vary by using chopped asparagus or green beans, or use a mixture of vegetables and greens.

BEET SOUP

3 medium beets, peeled and chopped
2 large carrots, peeled and chopped
1 medium onion, chopped
2 large potatoes, diced or cubed
2 stalks celery, chopped
4 cups salt-free chicken or vegetable broth
1 Tbsp. olive oil
3 cloves garlic, crushed
1 Tbsp. fresh grated ginger (optional)
Bragg's Liquid Amino Acids
pepper

In a large soup pot, heat olive oil, and then add onions and garlic (and ginger if you're using it). Sauté until lightly browned. Add carrots and celery and let the mixture cook for 5 minutes over medium heat. Add the beets and potatoes and cook for 5 more minutes. Add the chicken stock and bring to a simmer. Add the Bragg's and pepper to taste and simmer for 30 minutes.

BROWN RICE POLENTA

2 servings of prepared brown rice hot cereal
1 medium yellow onion, chopped

2 Tbsp. olive oil
2 cloves garlic, crushed

Sauté onions and garlic in 1 Tbsp. of olive oil until lightly browned. Add this mixture to prepared rice cereal. Form into medium size patties and brown in skillet with 1 Tbsp. olive oil, at least 5 minutes per side. Serve with Tomato/Basil Sauce.

TOMATO/BASIL SAUCE

1/2 medium yellow onion, chopped
2 cloves garlic, crushed
2 tsp. dried basil or 1/2 cup fresh basil
About 1-1/2 cups of diced fresh tomatoes.
2-3 cups fresh spinach (optional)

Sauté onion, garlic, basil (and spinach if used) in 1 Tbsp. olive oil for 5 minutes over medium heat. Add tomatoes and simmer for 10-15 minutes. Add salt and pepper to taste. (You could also serve this over chicken, or chill it and add it to salads.)

MUSTARD GLAZE FOR LAMB

1 tsp. dry mustard
1 Tbsp. Bragg's Liquid Amino Acids
1 clove garlic
1/8 in. slice ginger root, minced
1 tsp. crushed dried rosemary or 2 Tbsp. fresh
1/4 c. olive oil
lamb shoulder, leg of lamb or lamb chops

Combine mustard, Bragg's, garlic, ginger, and rosemary. Gradually whisk in olive oil. With brush, coat lamb thickly and evenly and refrigerate for at least 3 hours or overnight. Roast lamb in oven on rack.

LAMB KABOBS

2 lbs. ground lamb
1 tsp. ground cumin
1/8 tsp. cayenne red pepper
1/3 c. fresh cilantro, chopped

Mix all ingredients together. Let sit at least two hours. Make long flat kabobs on skewers and grill to desired doneness. Serve with brown rice cooked with fresh dill, 1 Tbsp. olive oil.

HERB-GARLIC MARINADE FOR CHICKEN, LAMB, OR SHRIMP

6 large garlic cloves
1/4 c. fresh rosemary leaves
1 c. fresh lemon juice
1-1/2 c. olive oil
1/3 c. packed fresh thyme sprigs
1-1/2 Tbsp. kosher salt
ground pepper to taste

Mince together garlic, thyme, and rosemary with salt and mash into a paste. Add remaining ingredients and whisk until blended. Marinate up to 1 day, covered. Makes about 2-1/2 cups.

CHICKEN MARINADE

1/4 c. Bragg's Liquid Amino Acids
1 Tbsp. curry powder
1 tsp. ground ginger
dash of red cayenne pepper
2 Tbsp. olive oil
1 tsp. cinnamon
1 garlic clove, crushed
2 broiler chickens

Mix together all ingredients. Clean chicken, remove as much skin as possible, and split chicken open to lie flat on roasting pan. Spread marinade on both sides of chicken, cover and refrigerate for 2 hours and up to one day. Bake chicken at 375 degrees until done.

CARIBBEAN CHICKEN WITH PINEAPPLE SALSA

Chicken:
2 large boneless chicken breasts
2 garlic, chopped
1/2 jalapeno pepper, chopped
1 large shallot, chopped
1/2 c. fresh cilantro
3 Tbsp. olive oil

1 tsp. kosher salt
juice of 1 lime

Salsa:
1-1/2 c. diced fresh pineapple
3 Tbsp. red onion, chopped fine
1/4 jalapeno pepper, minced
2 Tbsp. cilantro leaves, chopped

Puree all ingredients for chicken marinade and put in plastic Ziploc bag with chicken. Grill and serve at room temperature or warm.

Combine all salsa ingredients except cilantro together and refrigerate up to one day. Add cilantro before serving.

SUMMER CHICKEN SALAD

Dressing:
1 clove garlic
2 Tbsp. + 1-1/2 tsp. olive oil
1-1/2 Tbsp. + 1 tsp. lemon juice
1 T. almond oil
1 tsp. dried herbes de Provence
1/4 tsp. salt or to taste

Salad:
2 c. roasted chicken, skinned and chopped (can buy already cooked)
1 ripe mango, peeled, pitted and diced
6 c. mixed salad greens
1 avocado, peeled, pitted, diced just before serving

Combine all dressing ingredients and shake or stir well. Toss salad, mango and chicken together and mix with dressing. Garnish with avocados.

BEEF OR CHICKEN SKEWERS

1/2 c. Bragg's Liquid Amino Acids
2 Tbsp. lemon juice
1 clove garlic
1/2 tsp. ground ginger
2 Tbsp. olive oil

1 tsp. sesame seeds
2 green onions, finely chopped
1 lb. beef sirloin, thinly sliced or boneless chicken breasts

Combine all ingredients. Thread meat on bamboo skewers; marinate at least 3 to 4 hours or overnight. Broil or grill until meat is cooked through.

FLANK STEAK MARINADE

1-1/2 tsp. salt
1 Tbsp. minced onion
1/2 tsp. dry mustard
1/2 tsp. rosemary
1/4 tsp. powdered ginger
1/4 c. lemon juice
1/2 c. olive oil
1 clove garlic, minced
1/4 c. Bragg's Liquid Amino Acids
1 tsp. ground black pepper

Place all ingredients in blender and blend until smooth. Marinate overnight.

STEAK MARINADE (2 lbs. of flank steak or boneless sirloin tip)

1/2 c. Bragg's Liquid Amino Acids
1 Tbsp. garlic
1 tsp. ground black pepper
1/4 c. olive oil
1 2-inch piece of ginger, minced
2 tsp. ground coriander

Marinate steak 4 hours up to overnight.

MARINADE FOR BEEF TENDERLOIN

1/2 c. olive oil
1/2 c. chopped shallots
2 Tbsp. chopped fresh rosemary
8 (6-7 oz. beef tenderloin steaks, 1" thick)

Purée oil, shallots, and rosemary in blender until almost

smooth. Pour into 13x9x2 glass baking dish. Add steaks, turn to coat with marinade. Cover and refrigerate at least 6 hours or overnight. Grill to desired doneness.

BASIL AND SAGE STEAK

Dry Rub:
3 Tbsp. dried basil
1-1/2 Tbsp. sage
1 Tbsp. kosher salt
1 tsp. black pepper
4 steaks about 1 to 1 1/2 inches thick

Sage Sauce:
4 Tbsp. olive oil
1/4 c. packed fresh sage leaves
1/4 c. packed fresh basil leaves
1 tsp. mashed anchovy fillet or paste

Dry Rub:
At least 2-1/2 hours and up to 12 hours before you grill the steaks, prepare the dry rub combining all ingredients in a small bowl. Coat the steaks thoroughly with the rub, wrap them in plastic and refrigerate until 30 minutes before grilling. Grill to desired doneness.

Sage Sauce:
Combine oil, fresh sage and basil in small saucepan. Cook over medium heat about 10 minutes. Strain the sage and basil leaves, then add the mashed anchovies. Spoon sauce over grilled steaks.

STEAK WITH ROSEMARY AND TOMATOES

6 plum tomatoes, halved
12 garlic cloves, halved
1/4 c. olive oil
4 steaks (1-inch thick)
1/4 c. chopped fresh rosemary
2 Tbsp. ground black pepper
1 Tbsp. kosher salt
2 Tbsp. olive oil

Heat oven to 275 degrees. Combine tomatoes, garlic and olive oil in small ovenproof casserole, season with salt and pepper. Cook, stirring occasionally, 1-1/2 hours.

Rub steaks with rosemary, 1 Tbsp. pepper and kosher salt about 10 minutes before cooking. Cook steaks until desired doneness and serve with warm tomatoes.

RIB ROAST MARINADE

1 standing rib roast of beef
1 Tbsp. chopped fresh rosemary leaves
1 tsp. ground black pepper
2 garlic cloves
1-1/2 tsp. kosher salt

In a small bowl stir together seasoning. Put rib roast, rib side down, in a roasting pan, rub with olive oil and then rub seasoning mixture on the top and sides. Roast beef in lower third of the oven for 20 minutes at 475 degrees. Reduce heat to 350 degrees and roast until thermometer registers 130.

HAMBURGER OR GROUND TURKEY HASH

1 medium onion, chopped
1 lb. hamburger or ground turkey
3 eggs
1 Tbsp. olive oil
1 lb. fresh spinach
salt and pepper to taste

Heat oil in skillet and sauté onion until soft, about 7 minutes. Remove from pan. Brown meat until it loses its pink color, about 3 minutes. Add spinach and stir until wilted, about 2 minutes. Add onion and salt and pepper. In a separate bowl, whisk the 3 eggs together. Pour the eggs into the center of the pan and cook slightly before mixing with the rest of the hash. Continue cooking until eggs are done to desire.

SOUTH AMERICAN CHILI

2 Tbsp. olive oil
2 c. onions

2 c. chopped red bell peppers
4 large garlic cloves, minced
2 lbs. ground beef
1 Tbsp. cumin
1 14-1/2 oz. can beef broth
1 c. frozen peas

Heat oil in large pot over medium-high heat. Add onions, bell peppers and garlic, sauté 5 minutes. Add beef, cumin and cayenne pepper, sauté until beef is brown, breaking up beef with back of fork, about 8 minutes. Add crushed tomatoes, broth, peas, and capers. Simmer until chili is thick, stirring occasionally, about 20 minutes. Season with salt and

FISH MARINADE

2 lbs. snapper, trout, or flounder fillets
1 onion, thinly sliced
1/4 c. olive oil
1 tsp. sea salt
dash pepper
4 Tbsp. citrus juice (lemon, lime, grapefruit or any combo)
2 Tbsp. Bragg's Liquid Amino Acids

Place fish in oiled baking pan. Slash fish in several places and inset onion slices. Mix olive oil, salt, pepper, citrus juice and Bragg's. Spread over fish and baste during cooking. Bake 20 minutes, or until fish flakes easily with fork. (You can substitute 4 Tbsp. orange juice concentrate for citrus after adding it back to diet)

TUNA SALAD WITH BEEFSTEAK TOMATOES

2 cans white albacore tuna
2 tsp. drained capers
2 Tbsp. chicken broth
1 Tbsp. fresh lemon juice
1/4 c. mayonnaise
salt and pepper to taste
2 large, ripe tomatoes, slice 1/4 in. thick

Mix the tuna, capers, chicken broth and lemon juice in food processor. Remove and fold in mayonnaise. Season to taste. Cover and chill at least 1 hour. Slice tomatoes, sprinkle with salt and pepper, and serve tuna scoop on top.

FRESH TUNA WITH WATERCRESS SALAD

5 Tbsp. Bragg's Liquid Amino Acids
1/4 c. fresh cilantro leaves (packed)
2 Tbsp. mayonnaise (use homemade with lemon, it can't have vinegar)
1 Tbsp. sesame oil
2 tsp. lime juice
1 one-inch piece peeled fresh ginger (chopped)
1/4 tsp. cayenne pepper
2 bunches watercress (stems trimmed)
1 bunch radishes, trimmed, sliced (optional)

Blend first 7 ingredients in blender until smooth. Pour 1/3 cup sauce into glass pie plate, add fish and turn to coat, 15 minutes per side. Reserve remaining sauce.

Drain marinade from fish into heavy medium skillet. Cook over high heat until liquid starts to boil. Add fish and cook to desired doneness, about 3 minutes per side for medium rare.

Combine watercress and radishes in bowl, arrange fish slices over it, sprinkle with sesame seeds and reserved marinade.

SALMON WITH FRESH GINGER SAUCE AND RICE

Squeeze a lime over salmon and broil/grill to desired doneness. Serve with ginger sauce and rice.

GINGER SAUCE

1 (1/2-inch thick) ginger root, peeled, minced
1/2 c. mayonnaise (homemade with lemon juice and eggs)
2 tsp. chopped cilantro leaves
2 tsp. lime juice
1/4 tsp. hot chili oil

Combine all ingredients in a small bowl. Refrigerate until ready to serve.

PINEAPPLE, RED PEPPER BROWN RICE SALAD

4 c. cooked brown rice
1 Tbsp. + 1 tsp. olive oil
1 Tbsp. + 1 tsp. lemon or lime juice
1/2 tsp. salt
1/2 tsp. hot chili oil
1 c. diced fresh pineapple
1/2 c. diced red pepper
1/2 c. green onions with some top
1 tsp. sesame oil

Take 4 cups of cooked brown rice, stir in pineapple, transfer to bowl. Add lemon juice, chili oil, bell pepper, green onions and sesame oil. Toss to mix. Adjust seasonings with salt and chili oil. Best if served same day.

HERBED RICE PILAF

2 tsp. olive oil
1 large shallot, minced
1 c. brown rice
1 c. chicken broth + 1 c. water
3 Tbsp. minced fresh cilantro or parsley
salt and pepper to taste

Heat oil in small skillet, add shallots and cook until soft. Stir in rice, broth and simmer covered until done (or add all ingredients to rice cooker). Let stand 10 minutes and add cilantro/parsley.

GREEN HERB SAUCE (for baked potatoes, salmon, eggs)

2 lemons
5 garlic cloves, chopped fine
1 c. fresh cilantro, chopped
1 c. fresh basil, chopped
1/2 c. fresh parsley, chopped
1 c. olive oil
1 tsp. salt
1/2 tsp. pepper

Grate zest from both lemons. Halve and squeeze juice from them. Add garlic to lemon juice and zest. Stir in chopped cilantro, basil and parsley. Add the olive oil, stirring until blended. Add salt and pepper. Serve at room temperature.

ANOTHER HERBED RICE

1 tsp. dried onion flakes
1/2 Tbsp. dried celery flakes
2 Tbsp. dried parsley
1/2 tsp. dried garlic flakes
1/2 tsp. turmeric
1/2 tsp. sea salt
1 c. chicken broth + 1 c. water
pinch ground cloves
1 c. brown rice
1 c. chopped scallions

Combine all ingredients and put in rice cooker or cook according to rice package instructions.

FIVE-SPICE RICE

1 Tbsp. sesame oil
1 c. brown rice
1/2 tsp. sea salt
1 tsp. five-spice powder
1 Tbsp. fresh ginger, minced
1/2 c. chopped scallion
1 c. frozen peas, defrosted
2 Tbsp. Bragg's Liquid Amino Acids
1 c. chicken broth + 1 c. water

Mix all ingredients together in rice cooker or put in flameproof covered casserole and bake for 40 minutes or until liquid is absorbed.

VEGETABLE CASSEROLE

1/2 c. olive oil
2 cloves garlic, minced
1/4 c. fresh parsley
1/2 tsp. bay leaves
1-1/2 tsp. marjoram

1-1/2 tsp. red pepper flakes
2 large onions
1/2 acorn squash, peeled, cubed
1 eggplant, unpeeled and cubed
2 zucchini (yellow or green), 1/2-in. thick slices
2 peppers (red, yellow, green)
1 c. carrots
2 small red potatoes, quartered
1 small cauliflower, broken into flowerets
1-2 medium tomatoes, seeded and sliced
handful of grapes
1/2 c. frozen peas

(You can substitute any vegetable except spinach and beets)

Puree oil, garlic, parsley, bay leaves, marjoram, and red pepper flakes. Prepare vegetables. Layer a large casserole with heaviest or slowest cooking vegetables on the bottom, ending up with the onions on top. Sprinkle oil mixture between each layer. Do not add the tomatoes, grapes, peas until the end. Cook vegetables covered for 1 hour at 350 degrees. Add tomatoes, grapes, peas and 1-1/2 tsp. sea salt for 15 more minutes.

SPINACH WITH CRISPY SHALLOTS

2 Tbsp. olive oil
4 large shallots (sliced thin)
salt, pepper
1 10-oz. package fresh spinach
2 Tbsp. lemon juice

Heat 2 Tbsp. oil in skillet until hot. Add shallots and cook on medium high heat until crisp, stirring often, about 8 minutes. Remove from pan. Sauté spinach in skillet until wilted. (You may need to add more oil) Add 2 Tbsp. lemon juice, stir. Drain spinach. Salt and pepper to taste. Serve with crispy shallots on top.

PUTTANESCA SAUCE

1/3 cup olive oil
1 Tbsp. minced garlic
4 c. canned plum tomatoes, drained and chopped

1 Tbsp. fresh oregano, minced
1/2 tsp. red pepper flakes
2 Tbsp. drained capers
12 black olives, halved
1 2-oz. can of anchovies, drained and minced
salt
pepper
2 Tbsp. minced fresh parsley
2 Tbsp. minced fresh basil
1 lb. cooked brown rice

To a large saucepan, add the olive oil and minced garlic. Sauté it briefly. Then add the plum tomatoes, fresh oregano, red pepper flakes, capers, and black olives. Cover the pan and simmer the sauce for 10 minutes, then uncover and simmer 10 more minutes, stirring occasionally.

To the reduced sauce, add the anchovies, and season to taste with salt and pepper. Simmer 5 minutes longer to heat through and blend the flavors.

Sauce the rice in a large bowl. Sprinkle on the parsley and basil. Freezes well.

Yield: 4-6 servings.

CORDERO EN CHILINDRON
Lamb in Chilindron Sauce

1-1/2 lbs. boneless shoulder or leg of lamb, cut into 1-inch cubes
1 tsp. salt
freshly ground black pepper
6 Tbsp. olive oil
3 cloves garlic (I recommend increasing this to taste)
1 large onion, chopped (use more if you like onion)
4 large red peppers, cored, seeded and cut into strips
1 cup skinned and chopped tomatoes
2 tsp. paprika
2 pinches of toasted saffron threads, or 1 tsp. saffron powder
1 chili pepper, seeded and chopped (dried chilies work just as well)
10 ripe or green olives, halved and pitted (canned black olives do well)

Sprinkle the meat with the salt and pepper. Heat the oil in a flameproof casserole or large pan with the garlic cloves. Add the meat and fry until evenly browned. Remove the meat and set it aside. Discard the garlic, if a milder flavor is preferred.

Add the onion and peppers to the pan and sauté until they start to soften. Add the tomatoes, paprika, saffron and chili pepper. Return the meat to the pan, cover and cook very gently for about 1 hour or until the meat is tender, adding the olives about 10 minutes before serving. If the meat becomes dry during cooking, add a little water, but the dish should contain little liquid.

Transfer to a heated serving dish and serve immediately. Freezes well.

ROASTED POTATOES WITH BASIL

Russet potatoes
Olive oil
Basil
Thyme
Salt and pepper

Preheat the oven to 450 degrees. Quarter the potatoes into long wedges and put directly into a cold pot of water. Put the potatoes on the stove and heat until the water starts to boil. In a frying pan put enough olive oil to coat all of the potatoes and transfer them to the pan. Sauté for about 10-15 minutes, or until brown, adding the basil, thyme, salt and pepper to taste. Then put potatoes in a baking dish or roasting pan and put in the oven for another 10-15 minutes until the sides are crisp. Serve immediately.

My Experience with the LifeForce Plan

As I said before, I like to keep the diet fairly simple, although I appreciate men and women who enjoy cooking and have more "gourmet" tastes. My typical day on the plan begins with scrambling egg whites with beef or various vegetables, including tomatoes and potatoes. I may mix avocados and tomatoes together and eat it as a snack. I also use yams or sweet potatoes and various fruits as snacks.

I sometimes cook a large quantity of ground beef with vegetables, and use this concoction for breakfast or lunch. I may make soup just by boiling a fryer chicken to make a stock and then I add vegetables I have around. I also use organic frozen vegetable blends and add them to broth or ground beef. I'm from the midwest, so I tend to eat beef quite often. I find that beef stabilizes my blood sugar and I feel energetic throughout the day when I include beef in my diet. Dinner, either at home or out, usually is a steak or other meat and vegetables. (I usually simply pan-fry steak.) I also buy frozen organic fruit blends and eat a bowl of the frozen fruit, often as a dessert or an evening snack

As you can see, I don't spend a great deal of time cooking. Like you, I find that shopping and cooking for the LifeForce Plan is very easy. Most of my patients are surprised by how easily they can adapt the plan to their schedules. After a few days, it doesn't seem like a "special" way to eat at all. I know if you give it a try, you'll discover that, too.

Resources

Supplements for The LifeForce Plan

All products are available at www.lifeforceplan.com or through the LifeForce Center at (888) 236-7780.

WWW.MCCOMBSxPLAN.COM

Thorne Research: 800-228-1966. (This company also produces a good hypoallergenic supplement line.)

Klaire Labs: 800-533-7255/www.klaire.com. (This company also produces Cal-Assimilate Plus and Multi-Mineral Complex.)

Digestive Support
Enzymes, Transformation Enzymes: 609-636-3607

Acidophilus, Jarro-Dophilus, Jarrow Formulas: 800-726-0886

Colon Program, Eden's Secret: 800-952-7873

Sonne's #7 & #9 (intestinal cleansing products) Peterson's Health: 800-433-7395

Vitamin E
Unique E, A. C. Grace: 800-833-4368. (This company produces the best vitamin E currently available.)

General Supplements
Country Life: 800-645-5768. (This company is a good overall producer of high quality nutritional supplements.)

New Chapter Vitamins: 800-543-7279

Royal Jelly
Premiere One Royal Jelly: 800-373-9660

Herbal Products
Herbal Magic: 800-684-3722

Miscellaneous Nutritional Products
Immunocal, Immunotech Research: 450-424-9992

Calorad and Agrisept-L, Essentially Yours, Inc.: 604-596-9766

Personal Care Products
Soaps and shampoos and household products, Five Star Soap
Products: 510-638-7091

High quality shampoo and lotions: Organic Excellence Products:
800-611-8331

Toothpaste, mouthwashes, deodorants: Desert Essence. (These
products are widely available in natural food stores. Desert Essence
is one of Country Life companies.)

Home Environment
Fred Van Liew's Essential Water and Air: 800-964-4303

Books

*Beyond Antibiotics: 50 (or so) Ways to Boost Immunity and avoid
Antibiotics:* Michael A. Schmidt, Lendon H. Smith, and Keith W.
Sehnert (1994, North Atlantic Books, Berkeley, California)

*Nontoxic, Natural, and Earthwise: How to Protect Yourself and Your
Family from Harmful Products and Live in Harmony With the Earth.*
(Unfortunately, this book, originally published by Tarcher, is out
of print. However, second hand copies are available on various
Internet sites.)

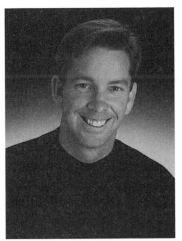

Dr. Jeffrey S. McCombs, D.C., is a third generation graduate of Palmer College of Chiropractic (1984). He is licensed in the states of California, Illinois, Colorado, and Arizona. He is a member of the California and Illinois Chiropractic Associations, the International Association of Specialized Kinesiologists, and the American Holistic Health Association.

Dr. McCombs developed LifeForce which is a detoxification and dietary

Kim Jew Photography

plan that counters the detrimental effects of antiobiotics and reestablishes the normal body flora, detoxification pathways, and regeneration cycles of a vital, youthful, and healthy body.

A dynamic speaker on national and local radio shows, Dr. McCombs also consults with patients and doctors all over the United States on chiropractic care, nutrition, diet, homeopathy, and herbs. He currently resides in Santa Monica, California.

His book *LifeForce: A Dynamic Plan for Health, Vitality, and Weight Loss* (Robert D. Reed Publishers) is available through Dr. McCombs' website: www.LifeForcePlan.com. His email is dr.jeff@lifeforceplan.com, and his phone number is (888) 236-7780.